Bill Clinton
C/O The White House
1600 Pennsylvania Avenue NW
Washington, DC 20500

Dear President Clinton:

We're sure by now the intelligence community has informed you of the upcoming masterwork <u>Baked Potatoes: A Pot Smoker's Guide to Film and Video</u>, due out from Doubleday next year.

We're currently soliciting guest reviews, and although you didn't inhale we thought perhaps you had a contact high and happened to be watching a film at the time and would like to author a guest review in our scholarly novella.

We know whoever is reading this will think it's a joke and we assume your aides will advise against our proposition, but think about it: A huge percentage of the populace gets high. Pot smokers have become a powerful and underrated crop, a demographic who can really make a political impact, assuming they are bused to the polls. We've thought a great deal before writing you, we've watched <u>The War Room</u> (incidentally, why is Paul always wearing shades?), we've even contacted President Reagan, but we're afraid he misplaced the letter.

In exchange for your review, our slogan will forever be "Bill's Our Bud." We know it doesn't knock you over, but that's just the kind of anti-marketing marketing that masquerades as sincerity and effectively brainwashes most of the electorate. We hope you or the First Lady will consider our offer. Chelsea never has to know.

Sincerely:

<u>Baked Potatoes</u> Authors
John Hulme
Michael Wexler

A Pot Smoker's Guide to Film and Video

John Hulme and Michael Wexler

MAIN STREET BOOKS

Doubleday   New York London Toronto Sydney Auckland

A Main Street Book

PUBLISHED BY DOUBLEDAY
a division of
Bantam Doubleday Dell Publishing Group, Inc.
1540 Broadway, New York, New York 10036

Main Street Books, Doubleday, and the portrayal of a building
with a tree are trademarks of Doubleday,
a division of Bantam Doubleday Dell Publishing Group, Inc.

Baked Potato logo by Gideon
Dedication page art by Ted Pryde

Library of Congress Cataloging-in-Publication Data
Hulme, John.
Baked potatoes: a pot smoker's guide to film and video / John
Hulme and Michael Wexler.
p.   cm.
1. Motion pictures—Catalogs.   2. Video recordings—Catalogs.
3. Drugs and motion pictures.   I. Wexler, Michael.   II. Title.
PN1998.H75   1996
016.79143'75—dc20   95-44224
CIP

ISBN 0-385-47837-2

3 5 7 9 10 8 6 4

Book Design by Claire Vaccaro

GRAFFIX

©TRI-CORP 1990

Contents

Preface

We lied to the casting agent to get the job: band members in the film *Radioland Murders*. John was a master of the stand-up base. Mike played the trombone. At five in the morning we exited the house, got in a shit-brown 1982 Cadillac, and drove to the studio. George Lucas had arrived to direct the end of the film, and there was a "buzz" on the set. Grips and electrics chowed breakfast burritos and bacon and eggs off the catering truck.

We got in line, moving with incredible patience, just a hand's reach away from victory, from the steaming vats of hash browns, biscuits, omelettes . . . and then it crumbled. A production assistant had spotted the advance, kindly removing us from the procession and directing us toward the extras' tent. Ah, it was only a matter of moments before we would once again gaze upon our bright-eyed colleagues. A potpourri of senior citizens, idiots savants, hopeless aspiring actors, and genetic mutants, puncturing and drop-kicking each other over a table of glazed doughnuts and water. All dressed in 1930s-period attire.

Opening the flaps of that tent was a moment that cannot be explained. Suffice it to say that there come those points in life when you get a dose of perspective, look around, and ask yourself the big question: How did I end up dressed in turn-of-the-century formal wear in a tent in North Carolina, baked out of my mind, and about to be exposed as a bogus big-band musician?

It was on that day, in the parking lot of Carolco Studios in Wilmington, North Carolina, at five-thirty in the morning, that we hit rock bottom. But it was also on that day, in the midst of the chilling ennui, that we resolved, once and for all, to conjure the idea that would spring us, forever, from the impoverished, Kraft-macaroni-&-cheese lifestyle of doom.

The concepts were remarkably crisp, considering the circumstance. Plans for a roving troupe of bingo operators, foraying amongst the extra tents and hosting games for the bedraggled masses. A long-needed innovation designed to alleviate the stress of watching other guests eye your previously claimed cheeseburger at summer cookouts—Burger Flag, small, golf-course-looking toothpick flags with all the major names printed upon them, simple and ready to stick in your burger once you throw it on. Imagine, your burger, grilling away nicely with a little BILL or JENNY flag in it. Go ahead, have a game of softball, taunt young infants, sneak into the woods and masturbate. Your burger is safe.

And there was one other idea: an extremely high concept for a book that no one would publish. A book for all our friends and roommates, the couch-ridden and irreparably baked. A book that reviewed movies in terms of their quality when seen high.

The bingo troupe wore off after we stopped smoking bowls. Burger Flag still seems to make sense somehow. But the *Baked Potatoes* thing had potential. We typed up a proposal, sent it to an editor we knew at Doubleday, and waited for the reply. A year ago, we had assembled a collection of short stories with him, and this new idea really upped our stock as literary hopefuls.

They liked it, but were tentative. Was it legal? Wasn't the whole country into this "say no to drugs" thing? How are the "couch-ridden and irreparably baked" going to get up and buy the book? This last one was an especially good question. "Couch-ridden" is not the market you are going for when writing your book proposal. Shit. They wanted evidence that there was broad support for the cannabinoid cause. Cheech and Chong? Signed assurances from this girl who lives in our garage? The president got baked? They would think about it and have a decision on Friday.

Well, this was a victory in and of itself and certainly one worth celebrating. We got high, paced around the house, and fantasized about the possibilities. Finally, a chance to skewer every no-talent hack in the country for all to see. A chance to call out the bad-seed shwag films of all time and venerate the true masters. A chance to expose the travesty of a ruse of a sham that the whole evils-of-pot paranoia really is. *Attention America:* Everyone gets high! Our roommates looked on with a great sense of pity.

At three P.M. that Friday, the phone rang and we got the news. We had been removed from the band. It wasn't our playing; they just wanted to take a different musical direction. An hour later, Doubleday called and gave us the nod. How does it feel to be sitting in your living room at four P.M. and someone calls to publish your pot book? Quit your job, get exceedingly baked, call your parents and hang up when you realize what you're about to say. Then get baked. Good-bye Dominoes Pizza! Good-bye golf caddie! Screw you, world. It's time to get fried and watch movies for a year!

Baked Potatoes was a reality.

Introduction

Deep in the divots of the Idaho plains, deep in the shantytowns of scholarship and academe, tucked away in the nameless hovels and musty corners of urban dystopia, a highly evolved breed of proud, warrior vegetable slowly grows and ferments.

They are immune to the bellicose forces that surround them: the unfriendly climate, weight lifters in Chevy Caprices, the unrelenting truckloads of cultural manure.

Mr. Mayor, there's a juggernaut in town that can no longer be ignored. It's not the high school band. It's not the molester in the phys ed department. It's not Drivers Against Drunk Mothers. Mr. Mayor, this is no bake sale. It's the Baked Potatoes.

Where once we saw MY CHILD IS A POPE JOHN PAUL HONOR STUDENT let us now see MY CHILD IS FRIED. Where once we received the President's Award for Physical Fitness, let us now demand the President's Award for Pasty Disrepair. Where once we saw random drug testing, let us now bear witness to random non-drug testing, in which sober employees are systematically weeded out and dismembered. These are family values for the *whole* family. This is our contract with America!

Ah, but there's so much more to drugs than life. There's film. And it is here that our story truly begins. From reliable sources like *Willy Wonka and the Chocolate Factory* and *Apocalypse Now* to unsung heroes like *Story of Ricky* and *Gates of Heaven*. From risky *Platoon*-like calls to lethal *Hudson Hawk* bad seeds, *Baked Potatoes* advises and consents, sacrificing all class and common decency to review and rate movies as to their true quality during a marijuana-influenced viewing.

Who hasn't racked his or her brain at home or in the video store, often for a pathetic length of time, revealing in blatant clarity their extreme bakedness, only to rent *The Beastmaster* for the eighteenth time? Who hasn't boggled his or her vegetable head for that elusive perfect choice, that compelling film forgotten or unseen in ages? Intensity, visual precision, sizzling wit, a quirky sensibility without the word *quirky* —these are the qualities that make a film a stoned or sober delight.

Baked Potatoes attempts what none before has even dared: to pack two bowls at once, giving serious and occasional pot smokers a road map for their all-important movie travels and ordinary folk a humorous tome of videos to explore. Unfortunately, it didn't work, ending up completely twisted and bizarre, thereby alienating all but the first half of the first category.

Fear not. While some assert this lifestyle kills brain cells, think of those that survive, how much stronger and smarter they are. Overall, you're in the black. Take the profits and reinvest in *Baked Potatoes*. You deserve it. Enough scaling through sober throngs of Blockbuster hell. Enough *Chips* reruns. *Baked Potatoes* goes to market and brings home the bacon.

Sure, you'll need the occasional temp job or late-night mugging of the elderly, a sporadic lung procedure or bout with insanity, but beyond these petty mites, *Baked Potatoes* strives, in earnest, to serve your every need from the prisonlike comfort of the couch. Passionate guest reviews and blinding cultural insights. Crucial irrelevant information and vital bibliographic data. Troubleshooting procedures for the risky calls gone awry.

It is but the tip of the bakedberg, a crystalline palace whose tenants we are proud to present to you at this time. Ladies and gentleman, please welcome a select battalion of friends, neighbors, passersby, and broiled human shells who rose to the occasion called *Baked Potatoes:* the devoted elders of the Baked Potato Advisory Committee (BPAC), the fast-lane brain children of BP Development, the BP General, the civil libertarians of the BP Legal Defense Team, BP Merchandising, the BP Foreign Lobbyists, and the BP Whipping Boy, humble and devoted entities with whom you will soon sojourn.

We've been arrested twice, removed from places of residence, alienated from family, politely asked to leave more than one video store (fuck you, Frank), confronted with abject poverty, and reduced to pastalike brain activity. All in the debilitating but heartfelt effort to forge a baked world of cinematic skunk.

Lo, when we are called upon to accept this challenge, to put aside a full roster of employment and community-service opportunity in favor of the Lord's work, so we must obey. We can only hope this text provides some small pleasure to the pot smokers and film lovers of the world, the stalwart but oppressed philosopher kings and queens of our time. Some condolence to the alleged wasteoids who have been shunned, locked away, and generally denied their rightful places on the great chain of being.

All we can pledge is that each film was screened in the proper state of mind and with the health and prosperity of baked individuals of foremost concern. All decisions thought out to the best of our abilities. All monies donated to shady, hedonistic causes.

Break free of your shackles and come out of the basement! Rent the appropriate films and go back. *Baked Potatoes* awaits your command. John Grisham? Ha! We buy and sell five Grishams before you clear the chamber. Poe? Misses by one letter. Twain? Wouldn't even put his real name on it.

With over 70 percent of Americans saying they have tried marijuana and 65 percent asserting they watch films regularly, *Baked Potatoes* appeals to 135 percent of the market, more than any other book to date.[1]

In the words of T. S. Eliot: "In the end of all exploring we shall return to the beginning and know the place for the first time." Used properly, *Baked Potatoes* should definitely accomplish this task.

Pulitzer Prize? Maybe. Great gift for grandma? Debatable. Your loyal film companion? Without question.

Baked Potatoes: healthy, satisfying, delicious.

[1] Numeric data is false.

Using Baked Potatoes

How to Use This Book

Get high. Read movie reviews.

Baked Potato Rating Scale

= Bad seed. Toxic. May result in permanent dysfunction.

Risky call. Could go either way.

Between risky call and four leaves.

Four leaves.

High art. Masterpiece.

The Key

= Best watched alone.

= Brain wave required: May demand concentration/baseline intellect.

= Good couch seat mandatory.

 = Best watched as daytime choice.

 = Feel-good movie.

 = Group effort recommended.

 = Harry Dean Stanton.

 = No brain wave required. All welcome.

 = Best watched as nighttime choice.

 = Subtitled.

 = Danger. Movie may cause emotional trauma.

 = That certain je ne sais quoi.

The Distributors (See Appendix I)

𝔇 = Available from Dave's Videodrome.

𝔽 = Available from Facet's Video.

𝓗 = May be hard to find.

𝒱𝓛 = Available from Video Library.

𝒱𝒮 = Should be available at your local video store.

I.
The Goes-
Without-
Saying List

In the tradition of "blank page" and "do not write here," Baked Potatoes proudly presents "The Goes-Without-Saying List." Clearly there exists a group of classics that anyone who's reading this already knows are essential. They need no review. Hence, they "go without saying," although you will find that some get reviewed anyway, 'cause in a pot book shit doesn't really have to make sense.

Printed below are but a handful of these classics. If you have not absorbed them fully, you may not be ready to embark on the journey at hand. Be patient and amass the necessary tools before proceeding. Beware: The ill-prepared shall encounter untold dangers.

Airplane!
Apocalypse Now
Blade Runner
Blazing Saddles
The Blues Brothers
Caddyshack
Cheech & Chong's Up in
    Smoke, Next Movie, Nice
    Dreams
Close Encounters of the
    Third Kind
Die Hard
Fletch
The Godfather, The
    Godfather, Part II
Jaws
Monty Python's Holy
    Grail, etc....
National Lampoon's
    Animal House
National Lampoon's
    Vacation
Pink Floyd—The Wall
Raiders of the Lost Ark
Slap Shot
Star Wars, Episodes IV, V,
    VI (the trilogy)
Stripes
The Terminator
This Is Spinal Tap
Total Recall
Bloodsport

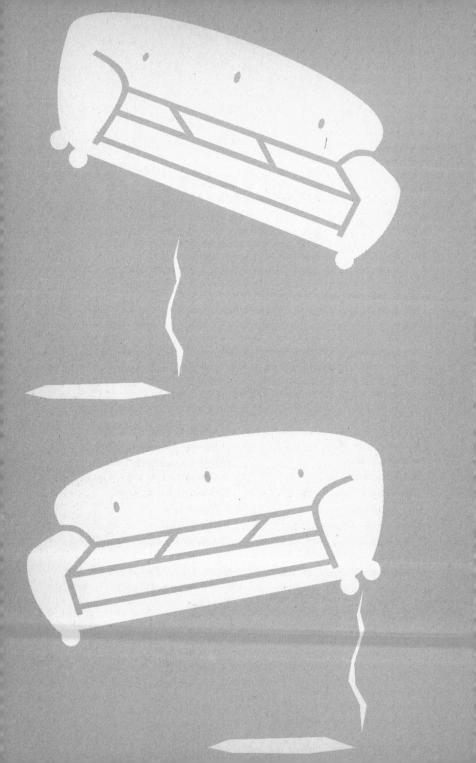

II.
Reliable
Sources

Certain things never let you down. American Gladiators. Shark Week. David Brinkley.

In a world of constant change it's vital to have reliable sources. Especially when you realize that the people who supply you are like you and therefore can't always preserve the goods necessary to supply you.

A dealer you can count on is like a treasured film ... a reliable source. Included here are many of the BP staples. Some you may have seen before, some you may have seen and forgotten, some you may have forgotten before you've seen.

Not in the mood for a blind date?

Wander the landscapes and lose yourself, then come home to papa.

The Adventures of Buckaroo Banzai Across the Eighth Dimension 🌿 🌿 🌿

The comic sci-fi escapades of America's favorite brain surgeon, inventor, rock star, savior of the planet, and all-around sensitive New Age guy.

Once upon a time there was a video game called Defender. It was the one that had so many buttons and display screens that it seemed to be designed with the Ray Milland/Rosey Grier creature in mind. No game gobbled up quarters quicker, with as much disdain for the player. Ah, but there was that one freak at every arcade, that computer cowboy who whipped up on alien spacecraft with the Zen aplomb of Mama Voorhees's only boy hacking his way through a campful of horny teenagers. He was the guy with the crowd gathered around him, the guy that brought a single quarter to the arcade, because he wouldn't need any more than that. He never said much, every now and then tossing a contemptuous laugh at the nimrods who'd mastered Zaxxon or Q∗Bert. And when they added the hyperspace button and changed the name to Stargate, he never batted an eye. He was a legendary figure of the eighties, who faded away into obscurity with Irene Cara, REO Speedwagon, and casual sex.

What does this have to do with *Buckaroo Banzai*? A valid question. This is a quality flick that's never received its due praise outside an already loyal cult following. The cast is superb, and the incoherent plot works in its favor. Like most good things, it's not for all the people. It's for the right people. The people who at this very moment are trying to figure why they are even attempting to read a book while stoned.

Buckaroo must not be forgotten like his kindred spirit and our hero, the Great Defender. Rent it in his memory, and try not to think what he might be doing with those hand-eye skills nowadays.

1984 (103 min.). Peter Weller, John Lithgow, Ellen Barkin, Jeff Goldblum, Christopher Lloyd. Dir.: W. D. Richter.

Alien
Aliens

You're having a nightmare, and something awful is chasing you.

There are a multitude of questions that enable you to find out if someone is cool. One of the best ones just might be "Which do you like better, *Alien* or *Aliens*?" If said person picks the former, chances are they're worth talking to. This is not to slam James Cameron's blistering sequel. Simply put, it's a lot harder to make a true horror film than a raucous action thriller. Ridley Scott's original touches on primal fears we'd all rather not acknowledge outside the safety of the local multiplex. And we don't mean those guys in the trees outside with the badges and infrared scopes. We're talking about those bad dreams you had as a child when you cried out for mommy and daddy and most of the time they would let you sleep in their bed but sometimes they wanted you to tough it out so they kissed you on the forehead and told you it was just a dream but you knew better because you understood what was in the closet under the bed just outside the window scraping the glass with its blood-encrusted claws and you swore that if you somehow survived until dawn and grew up to raise your own children that you would never under any circumstances force them to sleep with *Monsters* in their rooms!

Wanna thank your parents for their sensitivity? Send them a double-pack of *Alien* and *Aliens* and a bag of the Durban Poison. Remind them what it was like for you.

> Just for kicks, fast-forward to the part of *Aliens* when Bishop has been cut in half and Ripley opens the air lock to suck the alien queen out the door. As Bishop reaches to save the sliding Newt, catch a nice glimpse of Lance Henriksen's body standing in a hole below his fake android torso. Mayhap the greatest editing blunder of all time.

Alien: 1979 (117 min.). Sigourney Weaver, Tom Skerritt, Yaphet Kotto, Harry Dean Stanton, Ian Holm, John Hurt, Veronica Cartwright. Dir.: Ridley Scott.

    VS

Aliens: 1986 (137 min.). Weaver, Michael Biehn, Lance Henriksen, Bill Paxton, Paul Reiser. Dir.: James Cameron.

   VS

Alligator

Hormonally disturbed Chicago sewer alligator gone berserk.

You work, you go to school, you fart when no one can hear you or you're in a large room where proper blame cannot be allotted. Don't you love that? You're standing in a group and someone farts and everyone's just chattering on, drinking their cocktails, talking as if no one's farted. Occasionally someone will be like, "Oh, man, someone floated the heinous biscuit," but that only makes it worse. People begin suspecting one another, surreptitiously glancing around the circle, wondering who perpetrated the ugly bubble and knowingly plunged the group into the awkwardness of post-fart conversational syndrome (PFCS). Critics will lambaste us yet again for lack of class, but that's the price for tackling the hard-hitting issues.

Farts, call waiting, roadkill—with all that modern men and women encounter in a day, one forgets the simple pleasure of watching a fellow brother or sister devoured by a reptile. Sure, *Jaws* has its charm, but fish are beat; it's lizards that really pay the piper.

 Written by John Sayles.

1980 (94 min.). Robert Forster, Jack Carter. Dir.: Lewis Teague.

 𝒱𝐿 𝒱𝒮

Altered States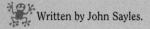

A scientist in search of the nature of humanity trips himself right back to the Stone Age.

We know this guy. Says he's tripped over a thousand times, and is looking for something he's never experienced before. So get this: He's paying thousands of dollars to ride a tiny boat loaded with safety gear and twelve other strangers into the heart of the Amazon, where they will meet a bunch of shamans from some tribe that still thinks Polaroids steal your soul. There they will consume countless amounts of some kind of tree fungus that will cause all takers to vomit for two to four hours. When that's over, they go on a trip so long and intense that without the shamans as guides there would undoubtedly be thirteen dead or ravingly insane tourists to explain to the American consulate. He's all excited. Can't wait to go lose his marbles in the jungle. Become one with the plants and animals and the elements and the shiny, drippy web of existence.

We'd be on the mind safari too, but we can't afford the boat pass.

Chances are neither can you, unless you take advantage of the amazing profit potential of *Baked Potatoes'* Appendix VIII. Of course, that'll take time, so where does that leave us now?

The only option is to rent *Altered States* and watch William Hurt go through the same thing on the tube. He doesn't get in touch with the animals. He becomes one, amongst other strange and visually stimulating transformations that you'll witness. Get a taste for the madness without becoming a part of it. It ain't the Amazon, but you won't need bug spray or shamans, and it only costs three bucks. Maybe next year.

Just in case you're inspired to rent anything else by the infamous British shockmeister Ken Russell? Forget it. The man's films collectively bring to mind a single, dominant image: an obese, sweat-soaked, naked man named Nathan, alone in his apartment, with one hand wrapped around his penis and the other around a box of cold pizza and watching the director's cut of *Reds*. Ugly. Sloppy. Excessive. Sleazy. Cheesy. Wheezy. Dull. Depressing. And generally unpleasant to the eye. Avoid especially *Gothic, Salome's Last Dance, The Lair of the White Worm,* and *Whore.* Our recommendation? Watch *Altered States,* don't take it too seriously, and skip the others. Unless you'd rather spend some quality time getting to know Nate.

1980 (102 min.). William Hurt, Blair Brown, Bob Balaban, Thaao Penghlis, Drew Barrymore. Dir.: Ken Russell.

Angel Heart 🌿 🌿 🌿

Sex, corruption, magic, and dead chickens in New Orleans, circa 1955.

When people get rich and famous they begin feeling like it's OK to indulge fantasies that the common spud represses. Baked Potatoes aren't afraid of a little role play. Sometimes we pretend we're scallions or snow peas, a turnip now and then, a giant spike-breasted dominatrix, a half-man, half-worm serpent, an eight-year-old transvestite concert pianist. Sorry. The point is, Mickey Rourke demands a gallon of fresh-squeezed watermelon juice in his trailer every day he's on the set. And never drinks it. What does he do with it?

Ask Robert De Niro. He hires Rourke, sending the sweaty sleuth on the trail of a missing singer, Johnny Favorite, into the worlds of the New Orleans occult, voodoo, Lisa Bonet. Blood drips, stew simmers, eye of newt, the question is moot.

Necromancy and seedy underbelly combine to form a Tropicana Twister that, unlike most, was actually meant to be. Even Rourke can barely stomach this acerb wafer. Not from concentrate.

1987 (112 min.). Mickey Rourke, Robert De Niro, Lisa Bonet. Dir.: Alan Parker.

      vs

The Beastmaster 🌿 🌿 🌿

Marc Singer, Tanya Roberts, and some jaguar-looking thing vs. minions of evil.

Every now and then a film emerges whose every component is weak. The actors are models, the story hinges on one boob shot, the fat kid next door does better special effects. Separately, each facet is embarrassing, but taken together and mixed with a proper dose of the hermetic, somehow, paradoxically, we arrive at clarity.

It happens. Take seven-layer dip: You don't want to break that down to its elements, but it tastes like gold. Take the government: Look at each senator and bureaucrat and president and you want to vomit. Combine them all in one city, get baked, and it's a comedy of the highest magnitude. Take a corn dog: Composed of hideous pork and beef slabs, corn meal, and deep-fried cow lard, but when assembled, again—beauty incarnate.

Sometimes the random combination of forces—God's work—is not fully clear until you get extraordinarily fried. Through this trapdoor, *The Beastmaster* reigns supreme and rules the jungle with an iron fist. You're embarrassed when you put it on the counter, but a true video-store worker will also be baked and give you that knowing "You're renting *The Beastmaster,* which the bald guy behind you doesn't understand, but we both know" look. "We know that we're both baked and I'm the video-store dude and you're the baked rentee. Two archetypes consummating the charter of their sacred constitution."

A metaphor. A cable classic. Eminently watchable.

1982 (118 min.). Marc Singer, Tanya Roberts, Rip Torn. Dir.: Don Coscarelli.

    VS

Better Off Dead 🌿 🌿 🌿 🌿

Breaking up is hard to do, but it was never this hard.

You've got the giggles. No point in fighting it. Here they come and there they go and here they come back around the mountain. Yes, the two people over your shoulder know you're high, and that's because normal people don't smile like you do for that long. That grin's about to slice your head in two. They're making side comments to themselves and it just won't go away no matter how hard you try and the reason it won't go away is the fact that you are aware the reason you can't make it go away is due to how baked you are. Charred. Laid over on a newly cleaned gas grill with shrimp, and barbecued. And it's not ending anytime soon. Everyone here knows that.

Your only hope? Find a safe place to deposit your overflowing laughter in a controlled, deliberate manner. The perfect remedy? A film that will keep you giggling from start to finish, which never hits too high nor too low. This film delivers the goods. Follow John Cusack and his hardships after his girlfriend dumps him for that evil Aryan kid who lurks in all movie high schools. Look back fondly on the days when every day was a crisis, and your parents just couldn't relate to your problems. Still the case today? Even better. You might want to push it—go for the risky call in search of the spectacular heights? It's your choice: Would you prefer to jump over the edge of the bottomless precipice in search of ultimate knowledge or grab your hang glider so you can enjoy the view at a more leisurely pace?

Trust those who know. Either way, you're *Better Off Dead.*

P.S. Don't forget to pay the paper boy.

1985 (98 min.). John Cusack, David Ogden Stiers, Kim Darby, Diane Franklin. Dir.: Savage Steve Holland.

Bill & Ted's Excellent Adventure

Uh, tomorrow's my history presentation and I'm baked and staring at a tank of fish.

When you had an exam you either cheated or failed. That's life. But in the movies George Carlin shows up with a time-traveling phone booth. Always wanted to prank-call famous figures in history? "Bruce? Yeah, man, just wanted to tell you . . . that movie you're about to do, *Hudson Hawk*? We're all really psyched about it here at Sundance. Seems like an important film." Click. "Moses, this is Aaron and Benjamin. We're baked, man, and we're in the Promised Land. Yeah, it's really sweet in here. No more of those Egyptian taskmaster dudes. How's the desert? You still hitting that rock instead of waving over it? Just kidding, man. Later."

Time travel meets potheads. What a great concept. If on the day you bought this book and we found out your name and found out where you lived and exactly when you first smoked pot while reading this book and then went back in time and told the cops you'd be getting high on this particular day and time and told them the exact time to burst in and bust you with a large enough of a controlled substance to invoke state mandatory-minimum laws that were long ago denounced as pathetic and we knew it was a large enough amount because we stashed a big bag underneath your couch on a day and time when no one was in the house and told them when to break the door down and physically carry you to the station and lock you up for good which is exactly thirty seconds from now when you go to jail and we come back in the house and loot your growing system hidden in the backyard and harvest all your buds and fall into the delusion of writing a pot book and somehow get a publisher to publish it and write a review of *Bill & Ted's Excellent Adventure* because it has to be in the book that ironically enough you read five seconds before you are carted off to jail where a crack addict hides under a mattress peeking his head out sporadically and claiming he's a turtle and telling you Paul Bunyan stories for eighty-six straight hours until your inevitable suicide.

Bye.

1989 (90 min.). Keanu Reeves, Alex Winter, George Carlin. Dir.: Stephen Herek.

   VS

The Breakfast Club 🍁 🍁 🍁 🍁

Is it normal to hate Emilio Estevez for no reason?

The Breakfast Club is kind of like your one emergency bong hit that you hid in your closet. You knew it was a good idea. You knew it was good pot. You knew you'd forget it existed. Then one day you put on that Wonder Woman suit, looked in the mirror, and boom, there it was, right under your golden lasso. Now, let's leave Lynda Carter out of this, because she's into contact lenses. She has a new life now and definitely didn't expect to end up here in *Baked Potatoes*. But then again, who did?

What is relevant is this impressive study of eighties teen culture. Five students from varying factions of a Chicago high school convene for a day of detention. Molly Ringwald before everything went haywire, Ally Sheedy, Emilio Estevez, Anthony Michael Hall, and Judd Nelson (last sighted in Arctic weather outpost searching for Timothy Hutton).

The Breakfast Club hits you with three soft lenses: the film itself; the commendable joint-smoking scene within; and the sensations and memories your baked mind revisits you with. Don't be afraid, it's just Uncle Bud in the clown suit.

1985 (97 min.). Ally Sheedy, Molly Ringwald, Judd Nelson, Emilio Estevez, Anthony Michael Hall. Dir.: John Hughes.

   vs

Cheech & Chong's Up in Smoke 🍁 🍁 🍁 🍁 🍁

Baked individuals on quest for quality product.

The first thirty minutes of *Up in Smoke* may be the best film sequence in Baked Potato history, possibly in the history of art as we know it. However, its greatness provides us with a conundrum nearly as boggling as it is humorous.

Is it possible that Cheech and Chong can really be acting this well, or is this movie actually an improvised skit by two thoroughly baked comedians? But if they were high, how could they possibly maintain their composure long enough to be intelligible on camera? But if they weren't, how could they pull off these scenes with that authenticity? But if they were, how could they have the patience and stamina for the endless hours it takes to shoot even the most standard of scenes? But if they weren't, how could they have the spontaneity that so obviously permeates the performance?

In summary, is it possible that two fried, Mexican-looking burnouts are the creators of the funniest thirty minutes in visual history?

The answer: yes.

> After the first thirty, things get tougher. A girl sniffs Ajax and speaks in tongues. Hard-hat area.

1978 (86 min.). Richard "Cheech" Marin, Thomas Chong, Stacy Keach, Tom Skerritt. Dir.: Lou Adler.

   vs

GUEST REVIEW

Reviewers:
Ben & Jerry
Occupation:
Ice cream guys

Attention: Neither of us have smoked any illegal substances nor do we ever intend to. What is this "baked" thing anyway? We don't do baked or fried; we're in the frozen end of things. Chilled, yes. I believe there is a slim possibility we have been innocent victims of secondhand smoke or perhaps a slight contact high. But we're not responsible. Victims, we say. By the way, we don't watch movies either. We have once been in someone's house when a video was playing, but . . .

Cool Hand Luke 🌿 🌿 🌿

Sly con rebels against bogus prison injustice.

It's those bad guys again, trying to break the human spirit. They're sinister, they're mean, they've got guns and dogs and manacles, they can even stick you in the box. It's Authority with a capital *A*, and they're going to do whatever it takes to get you to follow the rules. Only this time they've come against Paul Newman, and he's got some problems with rules, it seems.

This is a great movie. Paul Newman is at his charming, rebellious, and hilarious best. George Kennedy is good enough to make us forget about some of his television roles. And the story keeps us tuned-in the entire way.

Much dialogue and many scenes from this movie have endured in our normal conversation, even after many years. They can try and try to beat you down. It can be pretty tough to fight the powers that be. Sometimes it's a lot easier to toe the line. But they can't get your soul if you don't let them. And you can have a good laugh along the way.

Sometimes this video is a little hard to find, but it's worth the effort. Try it with a little Cherry Garcia.

1967 (126 min.). Paul Newman, George Kennedy, J. D. Cannon, Harry Dean Stanton, Dennis Hopper. Dir.: Stuart Rosenberg.

    vs

Dazed and Confused

A day in the life of 1970s high school seniors.

Mikey got killed from Pop Rocks and soda. No one ever does a period piece on that. All you get is Vietnam, World War II, Lincoln and Kennedy, all these stuffy opera-singer guys.

What happened to the golden age, the seventies, when the infomercials had character? The Ginsu, the Ronco Glass Cutter, the Vinyl Repair Kit. You know the guy who did the Vinyl Repair Kit lived it. He was proud. He woke up in the morning and was like, I'm the dude who invented the Vinyl Repair Kit so go fuck yourself.

Linklater remembers. That's what *Dazed and Confused* is all about—

the late seventies, when high school was a Bamboo Steamer and dad looked like The Club.

You've got to be wary when people set up easels in BP territory. The last guy ended up painting that infinite painting of painters painting painters painting.

This follow-up to *Slacker* is a well-written, well-done little toke of a taste, however. Slater (Rory Cochrane) is perhaps the most accurate film depiction of the Baked Potato ever steamed.

Things are on their way back again, kids: The latest polls show 31 percent of college sophomores feel politics is important; 32 percent favor marijuana legalization. Election day? Break out the tai stick.

1993 (94 min.). Jason London, Rory Cochrane, Sasha Jenson. Dir.: Richard Linklater.

      VS

The Dead Zone 🍁 🍁 🍁

Granted psychic powers from a near-death accident, a man must choose between hiding or saving society from an approaching evil of which he is aware.

One of the BP staff who will remain nameless had an unfortunate experience a few years back. He received a bag of hydroponic Colorado pot in his college dormitory that was so insanely good he was forced to wrap it in twenty different boxes like one of those wooden Chinese dolls. He put it in his bottom dresser drawer, and when he returned later that day, the entire room was completely resinated.

Like a good student, he began smoking the pot on a regular basis, and it quickly became known on campus and in a number of other states as "the crazy." He was proud to have ushered it into the world.

About halfway into the bag, a friend named You're Screwed knocked on the door in the form of an inexplicable eye twitch that had developed every time he smoked the pot. He stopped. The eye twitch did not. He consulted campus health, who informed him that he had created a "dead zone" in the eye area that contributed to the twitching, and that it may or may not go away. There's not a lot of jobs out there for a twitching pot addict, let's put it that way. As fate would have it, he found his home at BP Merchandising, where he now hand-paints potatoes like Easter eggs and sells them to local field-hockey players and retired clergy.

Unfortunately, his dead zone was never a Stephen King tale, attracting the likes of Christopher Walken, Martin Sheen, and Tom Skerritt. His dead zone was never the topic of an underrated feature tracing Walken's struggle with disturbing visions of the future. His dead zone was never something you wanted to see high.

All he can do is take Chairman Pryde's sound advice and, in the tradition of smoking yourself sober, try to smoke till he powers through the twitch.

1983 (103 min.). Christopher Walken, Brooke Adams, Tom Skerritt, Martin Sheen. Dir.: David Cronenberg.

VS

The Dirty Dozen, and anything Alistair MacLean had anything to do with.

Men on a mission.

They're a team of experts in all the military disciplines. Demolitions. Hand-to-hand combat. Sharpshooting. Languages. There's an expert assassin who's lost the edge, and some random guy particular to the needs of each individual mission. All under the auspices of the crafty and brilliant strategist with a shady past. There's also a double agent in their midst, but they can't call off the mission. There's no time. Something big must be blown up before the good guys are screwed. The high command is counting on them. They blow away countless Nazis or Russians, get into unbelievable pickles and somehow weasel their way out. The testosterone level is very high, and there's a lot of unspoken respect that can only be understood by men who've gone to hell and back together. The kind of thing that drives Tennessee Williams's characters to contemplate suicide. Some of the best characters die, but that's OK, because they win in the end and democracy prevails.

They're the war games you played as kids, come to life on-screen. They didn't let you down in the backyard, and they won't tonight.

Especially look for *Where Eagles Dare, The Guns of Navarone, Force Ten from Navarone,* and *Ice Station Zebra,* and better toss in *The Great Escape* and *The Magnificent Seven* for good measure.

VS

GUEST REVIEW

Reviewer:
Steve Hager
Occupation:
Editor in chief, *High Times*

The Doors 🌿 🌿 🌿 🌿 🌿

Rock biography of The Doors.

Although former drug czar William Bennett thinks pot makes people stupid, chronic TV watching is a far greater culprit. Most people forget that TV is a drug, and when you mix drugs you get synergistic effects. Pot's a little different. Depending upon how it's used, it can be a sacred substance that brings us closer to the Creator. Which brings us to this fine film by Oliver Stone. In telling the story of one of the most influential bands of the sixties, Stone portrays Jim Morrison as a psychedelic shaman who breaks through society's barriers to make contact with a deeper spiritual universe. Peyote helps Morrison make this journey, but so does the primal energy of rock and roll. Straight, you might have trouble accepting it, but I saw this film on mushrooms and it blew me away. I've watched the video a few times at home and have found the music, message, and spectacle greatly enhanced by cannabis. Val Kilmer, whose portrayal of Morrison is uncannily real, tragically descends into hard drugs at the film's end. One of the greatest rock bios ever made.

1991 (135 min.). Val Kilmer, Meg Ryan, Frank Whaley, Kevin Dillon, Kyle MacLachlan, Billy Idol. Dir.: Oliver Stone.

 VS

Dr. Strangelove or: How I Learned to Stop Worrying and Love the Bomb 🌿 🌿 🌿 🌿

Nuclear annihilation is funny.

So we're not really scared of Armageddon anymore, are we? Once we sat tucked under the bed or desk, clutching the Book of Revelation and waiting for Wormwood to drop from the sky. Alpha and omega, the first and the last, tread His flaming, sandaled feet just around the corner. And now? The fall of communism has changed all that, right? We've got nothing to be afraid of . . . or do we?

Better throw in *Dr. Strangelove*, just in case. Let it remind you of what used to keep us awake at night. The scathing black humor has aged to a fine vintage, and Peter Sellers puts on a virtuoso show as three completely different characters. Special kudos must be bestowed upon Sterling Hayden, Slim Pickens, and a young James Earl Jones before he prostituted his baritone to the highest bidder. "This . . . is CNN." Cha-ching.

Enjoy, but be sure to keep a water bottle handy. Wouldn't want to risk losing those precious bodily fluids . . .

1964 (93 min.). Peter Sellers, Sterling Hayden, George C. Scott, Slim Pickens, James Earl Jones. Dir.: Stanley Kubrick.

  J   VS

Drugstore Cowboy

Close-knit junkies on quest to survive.

Something about *Drugstore Cowboy* is kind of sad. Not really tear-jerker sad, but kind of bittersweet sad, like a good "Peggy O." The writing, direction, and performances—all outstanding. The relationship between Matt Dillon and Kelly Lynch—utterly convincing. One of the most powerful and purest I-love-yous in recent screen memory.

Yet while the characters are heavy into it and knock off pharmacies for a living, the film's not really about drugs. At first this turned us off, but then we got high again. What we saw was an incredibly realistic portrait of four people and their travails in the sketchy world of just trying to cope.

What separates *Drugstore Cowboy* from the field is that it goes one step beyond what is required, one step beyond good, indulging a few carefully placed brush strokes of randomness: the hat on the bed, etc. . . .

It's not the super-smiley candy-man high, but it's got intensity, like there's something real hiding in your bag.

Based on a novel by prison inmate James Fogle.

1989 (100 min.). Matt Dillon, Kelly Lynch, James Remar, James Le Gros, Heather Graham, William S. Burroughs, Max Perlich. Dir.: Gus Van Sant.

VS

Easy Rider 🍁 🍁 🍁 🍁

Two hip dudes hop on Harleys and road-trip through America in the late sixties.

The bikes. The tunes. The hair. The American West. That crazy hipster lingo. A classic as timeless as it is timely.

There's only one danger: It's 3:45 A.M. and people on multiple couches are looking for an excuse to crash. But there go Fonda, Hopper, and Nicholson blazing across the desert as the sound track kicks in with "The Weight." Everybody in the room starts talking shit about "wouldn't it be great if we just loaded up a van right fuckin' now, got outta this damn town, road-tripped across the country, and saw the world for a change." This adrenaline rush lasts until the first person realizes his or her mistake and finds a perfectly reasonable excuse why he or she can't make the trip despite how much he or she really, really wants to go. It only takes one, and the rest of the crowd will usually crumble.

But every now and then, there's that one unbalanced *Easy Rider* fan, the one person we all pray is absent from the room. That sturdy individual who calmly rises in the midst of all the commotion and states plainly: "I'll drive!" Your bluff is called. There's nothing left to discuss. Pack your bags, and don't forget the road soda.

P.S. Stop the tape after the Mardi Gras sequence. Trust us.

1969 (94 min.). Dennis Hopper, Peter Fonda, Jack Nicholson, Karen Black, Toni Basil. Dir.: Dennis Hopper.

 VS

Enter the Dragon 🍁 🍁 🍁

Why does my stomach look like a pierogi?

Enter the Dragon ain't winning no Oscar. Especially from that bunch of crochet hounds at the Academy. But you know what? It doesn't really matter. You can get a good scarf at any department store. Wool, cashmere, cotton, Gore-Tex, Thinsulate, Pyrex, kymax, who the hell can keep track anymore?

When we were spuds, you wandered naked in the Arctic and didn't whine like a grape every time an extremity broke off. And neither did Bruce Lee. For God's sake, he kicked Chuck Norris's ass. Walker, Texas Ranger pummeled for all to see. Now if that doesn't get your blood pumping . . .

Skip the tai chi workout, you look like a schmuck, and settle in for Lee, hired by the Brits to seek out opium kingpins in Hong Kong. Don't worry, he's not after the stoners, he's dead. But the tradition lives on. High-pitched screaming, walloping martial arts, judo, tae kwon do, po ta to. Great for pre-karate-tournament training or getting really high on your couch with a bunch of inert sloths.

 Winner, 1973 retroactive "Hash Brown."

1973 (97 min.). Bruce Lee, John Saxon, Jim Kelly. Dir.: Robert Clouse.

 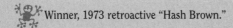

Evil Dead II:
Dead by Dawn 🌿 🌿 🌿 🌿 🌿

The horri-comic misadventures of filmdom's greatest hero and role model, Ash.

There's no way to do this film justice in the space provided. Don't think we didn't try. Reviews comparing *Evil Dead II* to the films of John Wayne, the French New Wave Movement, *Un Chien Andalou,* and the stories of H. P. Lovecraft have all been rejected by the necessarily harsh critical eye of the BP Advisory Committee. Why this abject failure by our crack staff? Perhaps it simply signifies that Sam Raimi's magnum opus should be stashed with the other so-called classics that some of the "team" decided we didn't need to put in the time to review, that group cop-out called the "Goes-Without-Saying List." Some USC film school guy goes off on a tirade about how YOU, our audience and readership, don't need to be reminded why the classics *are* classics, why you aren't interested in witty commentary dripping with drug-referenced double entendres and bizarre, look-how-much-acid-we've-taken-in-our-lifetime tangential anecdotes about films everyone already knows are great to watch when you're stoned! So the committee broke. Caved in to the pressure. Saved some space in the book for your favorite celebs or rock stars to put their two cents in to entice the star-gazing sheep out there to put their ten bucks in. So the list is there. Check it out. What're you missing? You'll never know, but one thing's for sure. Some of us will only cross the line of compromise so far. And the buck stops here, friends. A man like Ash, a film like *Evil Dead II: Dead by Dawn* will not be exiled to a laundry list of "Hey man, let's get fried and watch . . ." dinosaurs. It's bigger than that. Better than that. You're goddamn right it's getting its own review! Even if the space will only serve one of the writer's pathetic attempts to distance himself from his own multilayered corporate sell-out. So here it is. *Evil Dead II*. It doesn't get any better. Damn straight.

1987 (85 min.). Bruce Campbell, Sarah Berry, Dan Hicks, Theodore Raimi. Dir.: Sam Raimi.

 VS

Fast Times at Ridgemont High

Classic slice of life at Southern California high school.

The future must have something to do with the evolution of food sizes. Once there was large, medium, and small. Then there was huge, large, and medium. Now there's jumbo, huge, and large. Isn't there anything small left in the world?

Guess we shouldn't complain. What if the sizes were tiny, minuscule, and not-visible-with-the-naked-eye? "Yeah, can I get an invisiburger, two tiny fries, and a Coke droplet?"

Judge Reinhold in the pirate suit. That's what turned this toward fast food and *Fast Times*. Maybe it's lost a little magic with age. But think about how much it has. The mall, sex, drugs, music, Jennifer Jason Leigh, and Sean Penn as Spicoli, clearly one of the classic potheads in film history. He should be wrapped in foil and preserved.

A classic high school period piece, complete with Phoebe Cates and Mr. Hand himself. Archetypes. Legends. History. Based on the book by Cameron Crowe.

1982 (92 min.). Sean Penn, Jennifer Jason Leigh, Judge Reinhold, Robert Romanus, Phoebe Cates, Forrest Whitaker, Eric Stoltz, Anthony Edwards, Nicolas Cage. Dir.: Amy Heckerling.

   *VS*

Ferris Bueller's Day Off

"Please excuse me from school today. I have leprosy and am extremely baked."

Didn't you always want to call up the local radio station and report your school closed when it was snowing? Or even not snowing. Asbestos, hurricane, standard teacher suicide will do. In fact, we actually tried it. First of all, you need a numeric code to get the place shut down. Second, you don't realize it at the time, but an eight-year-old has a slightly different voice intonation than the school principal.

That's why *Ferris Bueller* is so damn infuriating. The kid (Matthew Broderick) was smarter than everyone, had a smokin'-hot girlfriend (Mia Sara), and a rich and easily manipulated best friend (Alan Ruck). What else do you really need?

Abe Froehman, sausage king of Chicago, Charlie "I'll Take Any Role with Four Letters" Sheen, and *Dirty Dancing*'s Jennifer Grey, Bueller's resentful sister who has continued (for no humane reason) to irk all of BP Central in every subsequent performance.

> 🎬☠️ New director's cut includes previously censored bong session right before day off.

1986 (103 min.). Matthew Broderick, Mia Sara, Alan Ruck, Jeffrey Jones, Jennifer Grey, Cindy Pickett, Edie McClurg, Charlie Sheen. Dir.: John Hughes.

 VS

First Blood 🍁 🍁 🍁

Vietnam vet harassed by pigs upon whom he wreaks ungodly (and fully entertaining) vengeance.

First Blood isn't trippy, it isn't weird, it isn't fancy. It's Stallone when you still had respect for him. Remember those days when Atari 2600 cost more than a hundred dollars? Action movies still had a remote chance of being good? Rocky Road ice cream was bigger than the pet rock?

Hard to say what it is, perhaps good filmmaking, but you find yourself really pulling for John Rambo in this trilogy opener. Someone once said, "There's only two stories that ever get told: Stranger comes to town and man goes on a journey." Well, this one is stranger comes to town with a twist: Town doesn't leave alive. That's right. Remember the charm of *First Blood*?

Finally, they have to fly in his old colonel to get the snafu under control. Richard Crenna arrives, gets face-to-face with the chief of police, Brian Dennehy, and delivers one of the great payoff lines in action-movie history.

This one's for those nights you want to eat steak, pretend to fix your car, and break shit for no reason. A good porterhouse, baked potato, and *First Blood*? Peter Luger couldn't do you better.

1982 (97 min.). Sylvester Stallone, Richard Crenna, Brian Dennehy. Dir.: Ted Kotcheff.

   VS

Flash Gordon 🍁 🍁 🍁

The intrepid quarterback of the New York Jets saves Earth from the evil devices of Ming the Merciless.

There are a lot of reasons why this film makes the cut. There's the immortal Sam J. Jones as the legendary sci-fi hero, who parlayed his first starring role into an illustrious career as a leading man in straight-to-video soft-porn thrillers. There's the unbelievably bad special effects that somehow work perfectly. And, of course, that rippin' Queen sound track. But none of this really matters, for *Flash Gordon* earned a space in *Baked Potatoes* for one reason alone.

Somewhere in this book, the unequaled genius of Topol had to be recognized.

1980 (110 min.). Sam J. Jones, Melody Anderson, Max von Sydow, Topol, Ornella Muti, Timothy Dalton. Dir.: Mike Hodges.

      VL   VS

Freaks

Shocking and monumentally unnerving account of 1930s circus freaks and their revenge upon the "normals" who torment them.

If you take anything from *Baked Potatoes,* if you rent one film this year, if you get one tiny joint to burn before you lose the battle with emphysema, burn it on *Freaks.*

This is before computer animation; these freaks are real. A torso who scampers around on his arms. Ogres. A man with no arms and legs who removes a match from a matchbox and lights a cigarette already in his mouth—*all in and with the other side of his mouth.* Think about that.

Rarely shown since it's 1932 release, banned in England for thirty years, *Freaks* has garnered underground status as *the* masterwork of twistedness. And it's not just ten minutes of genetic randomness; the story and direction are fully realized.

Anyone who fancies himself or herself a connoisseur of the bizarre, the macabre, the total mind-blow baked experience as a whole is but a human charade until *Freaks* is cataloged.

There'll be a point when you think you have to shut it off. Don't.

Also see *Dark Carnival: The Secret World of Tod Browning, Hollywood's Master of the Macabre* by David J. Skal and Elias Savada.

1932 (64 min.). Wallace Ford, Olga Baclanova, Leila Hyams, Roscoe Ates, Harry Earles. Dir.: Tod Browning.

From Russia with Love

Bond.

Dear Mom:

I took mescaline in Red Square today and I wanted to tell you something very important. It's not that I love you. It's not that I'm having the sea otter relapse again. It's that there's something Her Majesty has that we don't. That Q dude. Imagine what he could do on the right side of history? A growing system with a cloaking device. A self-rolling joint. Dogs that sniff out cops. Not that I get high.

But I digress. Q, shmu. Enough of the amorphous Caspar robbing phantasms; we've got Bond to discuss. Did you know that the second feature is considered one of the best, before they started stinking like Jason meets Bruce Lee meets lame soda-can pipe? Not that I get high. Fashioned in the image of his devotee herbivore audience, 007 has the style, the savvy, the presence of mind to thrive whilst the evil SPECTRE stalks his every samba.

Tied up with a Russian temptress/spy, Connery travels to Istanbul in search of a covert coding mechanism. I wish I could help.

Anyway, everything is good here. I think I've finally learned how to fly without bulky apparatus. Will try tomorrow from bell tower.

From Russia with love,

Jimmy.

P.S. Everyone here looks like Uncle Bud.

1963 (118 min.). Sean Connery, Daniela Bianchi, Pedro Armendariz, Sr. Dir.: Terence Young.

VS

The Graduate 🌿 🌿 🌿 🌿

Suddenly, I'm into Sade.

Some people run a marathon every morning. Some people eat fourteen meals a day. Some wash their hands every five minutes. Whether you're a heroin user or a marathon runner, it's about the same thing: transcending the normal plane of existence and looking for something more.

The trick, however, is to do both—to be a heroin user *and* a marathon runner. There aren't very many of them, but the few who excel are to be respected. All you hear about these days is how there aren't any role models and how society is crumbling. Well that's a crock. Show us a junkie who runs like the wind and we'll show you America.

Speaking of role models, meet Benjamin, home from college, aimless, lost, pathetic, and with a shocking resemblance to Dustin Hoffman.

For anyone living in mom's basement with a dugout and a VCR, you have arrived. It's 1967 and no one had a clue then, either. Except Buck Henry, who wrote a great script, and Simon and Garfunkel, whose sound track leads you to a bright-eyed future of older women, booze, and plastics.

Why can't you just go work in the mines like your father?

1967 (105 min.). Dustin Hoffman, Anne Bancroft, Katharine Ross, Murray Hamilton, Brian Avery, Marion Lorne, Alice Ghostley, William Daniels, Elizabeth Wilson, Norman Fell, Buck Henry, Richard Dreyfuss, Mike Farrell. Dir.: Mike Nichols.

    VS

Halloween 🍁 🍁 🍁 🍁

Kid takes fifteen-year stint in asylum, returns for razor-ingested mischief melee.

You could always tell the professionals from the dabblers. The pros had a pillowcase, a mission, traveling methodically as to never miss a dwelling. The rookies were often seen with parents. Moving with a casual, almost meandering gait. Immediately revealed by the tell-tale orange pumpkin.

When they grew up, the pros gave out Reese's. The losers gave out those abominable caramel cubes or, worse, Bit-O-Honey. And hence society split into these two realms, the pillowcasers and the caramel-giver-outers, the social yin and yang of modern civilization.

Halloween is no pear; let's put it that way. This one's a Krackel, a Mr. Goodbar. We'll go as far as a Reggie.

This flick hits you like a naked senior citizen giving out raisins. Off-guard. Shocking. You want to make it stop but you love it all the while.

1978 (93 min.). Jamie Lee Curtis, Donald Pleasence, Nancy Loomis. Dir.: John Carpenter.

   VS

Heathers 🍁 🍁 🍁 🍁

Ozzy Osbourne made me kill all my high school friends and eat live monkeys.

Names carry a lot of baggage. Look at Corey Haim and Corey Feldman. Similar to the riddle of how a toilet actually flushes is who in God's name still hires the Coreys? Sure, they've been around. Like to see them take on the Samoans or the Moondogs, though. Afa would do a number on those little punks.

Winona and Christian had a similar problem in this cynical, splendidly dark tale of assassinated teen queens. Not that their careers were headed for the WWF, but that the Heathers ruled the social scene. Until Ryder and outlaw boyfriend arrived to frame their suicides.

For those Baked Potatoes who have a few too many eyes, perhaps a slight deformation in elliptical genotype, shunned by farm children, you may sublimate vicariously through this vengeful catharsis. Geek.

It's not every day a movie has the balls to be twisted and well-done at the same time. Not since Lou Gossett and *Iron Eagle II*. Except that was neither.

Let's dole out some positive reinforcement for a solid eighth.

1989 (102 min.). Winona Ryder, Christian Slater, Kim Walker, Shannen Doherty. Dir.: Michael Lehmann.

👁 ♫   VS

Any movie starring Lance Henriksen 🌿 🌿 🌿

Action thrillers starring a man who speaks for himself.

The films read like underlined verses in a pot smoker's bible: *Aliens, The Terminator, Pumpkinhead, Close Encounters of the Third Kind, Stone Cold. Stone Cold*? *Stone Cold*. The characters? Bishop, Ed Harley, Chains . . . leaders all. Crafty. Hell-bent for leather. Irrepressible. Interchangeable. They're all the same man and Lance still manages to pull it off. You simply feel comfortable when he's on the screen. At ease. Safe. Especially when he's blindly facing death armed with nothing but rusty one-liners and poorly applied latex facial makeup. Maybe the occasional sawed-off twelve-gauge. And when it comes right down to it, what else do you really need on a night like this?

Also includes *Near Dark, Nightmares, Hit List, The Horror Show*. Does not include *No Escape*.

   ♫   VS

The Highlander 🌿 🌿 🌿 🌿

Contest between group of immortal swordsmen for supernatural prize known as the Quickening.

Crosscut between present-day Manhattan and sixteenth-century Scotland, Christopher Lambert and Sean Connery turn in sticky performances for all ages. Mom, dad, Jimmy, even Uncle Bud can disconnect the O_2 tank and revel in the occasional *Highlander* wake-and-bake.

Don't think senior citizens don't partake, because they do. Shuffleboard, Florida, chronic disorientation, giant green sunglasses? Enough to convict. Anyone who plays shuffleboard on a regular basis is heavily medicated.

Incidentally, a guy we don't know told us the following story about dealing in Florida: He charters boats, takes them out into the ocean to pick up the goods, and pays senior citizens five thousand dollars each to sit on lawn chairs and play mah-jongg all around the boat so the Coast Guard doesn't suspect anything. This could be your grandparents.

After an uneventful theatrical release, *The Highlander* has finally garnered a deserved cult audience despite incessant and appalling violations of the sequel clause (see *Woodstock*).

For everyone who's ever wanted super powers, knows Apache Chief's chant for getting big, or played Ultima (or Wizardry).

🌿🐸 The Baked Potato General has determined that watching *Highlander II* may result in a fetus resembling Larry King.

1986 (111 min.). Christopher Lambert, Sean Connery, Clancy Brown, Roxanne Hart, Beatie Edney, Alan North. Dir.: Russell Mulcahy.

5   VS

Hot Dog . . . The Movie

Breasts, intercut with skiing.

Certain more "refined" members of the BPAC remain convinced that educated, fried people everywhere do not enjoy this type of tripe. Naturally, we dissented, citing ourselves and our audience as an often lowbrow group of scholars. Despite heated debate, however, in which a number of resignations were tendered, it was deemed necessary to review *Hot Dog* with caution and the utmost of political correctness.

There are only two scenes in this movie. One allows viewers to examine a group of people engaged in spectacular, extreme skiing. The other reveals breasts; usually Shannon Tweed's. That is all.

If this is a problem, you will not like this movie.

If this is not a problem, you may now embrace the *Dog*.

1984 (96 min.). David Naughton, Patrick Houser, Shannon Tweed. Dir.: Peter Markle.

 *vs*

Jaws

Big shark mangles, dismembers local youths.

You always wonder what compels an already established actor to do a *SeaQuest DSV*. It's not the kind of thing where you get the script and it's a gritty, off-beat tale of Spanish transsexuals but the director ruined it on the set and it turned into a submarine series. It's the kind of thing where you get offered two million dollars, debate selling out or not, and realize you're definitely gonna sell out for two mil., so you better find something in the script you can pretend you believe in. Then you end up on an E! channel interview talking about how *SeaQuest* is an AIDS metaphor.

Don't you just hate that? How you watch E! and these actors are on there talking in all these serious terms about these movies you know are total crap. You know what we want to see? We want to see someone with the balls to get on there and be like, "Listen, Leonard, the movie really has nothing to do with the vicious cycle of urban poverty or the use of shadow in early John Ford, it's just an unabashed piece of shit that the producer offered me a lot of money to make. You know what I'm saying?"

But there's enough hate in the world. Let's talk about positive things. Like sharks. Like killing and mangling. What can you say about *Jaws*, though? It's kind of bigger than any review. Although this one's putting up a good fight. Roy Scheider, Richard Dreyfuss, Robert Shaw, Spielberg directs.

Goes without saying.

1975 (124 min.). Roy Scheider, Robert Shaw, Richard Dreyfuss, Lorraine Gary. Dir.: Steven Spielberg.

  VS

The Kentucky Fried Movie 🌿 🌿 🌿 🌿

A collection of comic shorts by the twisted geniuses that brought you Airplane! and An American Werewolf in London.

From the secret files of the United States Senate, with a little help from the Freedom of Information Act:

January 8, 1957

Senator
United States Senate
1st St. and Constitution Ave. NE   #OA5599
Washington, D.C.   20500

Dear Mr. Senator,

      As per our last conversation with Dr. Lazardo
and the Committee's instructions, here are the results of our
controlled study at the OSI facillity in Pottersville. I
think you'll be quite pleased with our findings.

      In case #24, certain subjects were admin-
istered a large dosage of marijuana through the inhalation of
a "joint" (Counterculture slang for marij. cigarette).
Subjects were classified by the letter M and a random #. A
second group of subjects was not allowed to "get stoned"
(slang for sense of well-being provided by inhaled marij.
smoke; see Graph #3B). Members of this group were given a
number along with the letter S ("square", slang for non-
user). The M's were then introduced to the S's on an
individual basis in a controlled environment. The following
anomaly emerged, witnessed by observing clinicians and later
confirmed during interview sessions with the M population.

      During all personal interactions between M's
and S's, both parties complained of random moments when
communications would utterly break down. During that span
of time, usually between 1-5 secs. in length, the interaction
seemingly progressed in one of two directions. An M would
recussitate the conversation by calling attention to the
problem with a simple question, usually something on the
order of "Excuse me, but what were we talking about?" This
happens any time before the first second of dead air. The
second, and more common conversational direction, would take
place when the "stoned" individual would fail to remember to
even ask the previously mentioned question, and begin to
obsess violently about the discomfort of the silence.
Between seconds 1 and 5, there would usually be an awkward
parting of the ways, with M's then experiencing a steady
period of depressive mood swings ("coming down").

      The cause of this failed attempt at social
interaction, and this is important, Mr. Senator, is a mental
phenomena which has been classified as Short Attention Span,
or SAS. This study found a definite correlation between the
effects of inhaled marijuana smoke, and SAS. Please refer to
the statistical differences between the S group, the M group,
and the control group on the SKMALT (Standardized Kessler
Mermory And Logic Test). You will notice that M's fail to

You know what's great for SAS? A bunch of really funny, really short comedy sketches. Like *The Kentucky Fried Movie.*

1977 (78 min.). Evan Kim, Bill Bixby, George Lazenby, Donald Sutherland, Henry Gibson. Dir.: John Landis.

  VS

King of New York

Drug kingpin with a social conscience.

One of the few films ever made that can be enjoyed on both ends of a high.

On the upward spike, it has more than enough guns, explosions, violent deaths, drug consumption, and hilarious one-liners to hand you a complimentary ticket for the Little Green Engine That Could. It's got heavy hitters with the expensive baggage you don't mind carrying. And most of all, it's got Christopher Walken, as ex-drug kingpin Frank White, returning to the scene of the crime with his own special brand of madness.

On the downward spiral, it fits the needs of both substages. The nonstop pacing can help you restore your sagging bake. And for those who've crossed the threshold of recovery? The subtle nuances of the acting and a suspenseful plot will allow you to skirt the impending doom of extensive introspection.

You're covered either way.

1990 (103 min.). Christopher Walken, Larry Fishburne, Wesley Snipes, David Caruso. Dir.: Abel Ferrara.

  ♪ VS

The Manchurian Candidate

A hero of the Korean War turns out to be a deep-deep-deep-cover enemy agent. So deep, even he doesn't know.

John Frankenheimer's complex Cold War classic is dangerously slow at times, but its convoluted plot still fascinates. It's like overhitting a nitrous balloon . . . confusing, but kind of fun somehow. Before we continue with this review, please get a deck of cards. Got it? Good. Shuffle the deck. Now then. How 'bout passing the time with a little solitaire. Yes? We'll wait.

Do you see the queen of diamonds? Good. It's nice to have you back on the team. Your tools are in the black box . . . where we buried it last time. You'll find the silencer quite adaptable. It should fit your needs for both short- and long-range targets. Your new working name is Dobbs. A driver's license and five hundred dollars in cash have also been provided. Be frugal. Any questions, you know who to call.

Please sanction the following: Jane Fonda, the writers of *Saturday Night Live,* Graham Nash, John Sununu, Tom Monaghan, the guy from the Sam Adams commercials, Todd MacFarlane, Tipper Gore (Al optional), Rush Limbaugh, and, most important, Larry King. And pump a few into Nixon's grave just to make sure that tricky bastard stays where he belongs.

You have two weeks to complete your mission. Use the cyanide tooth only in worst-case scenario. Good luck, #115.

1962 (126 min.). Frank Sinatra, Laurence Harvey, Janet Leigh, Angela Lansbury, Henry Silva. Dir.: John Frankenheimer.

  VS

Manhunter 🌿 🌿 🌿 🌿

Our introduction to the happy world of Hannibal the Cannibal and his serial-killing pals.

This prequel to *The Silence of the Lambs* has almost the same plot. Detective uses one serial killer to catch another, all the while putting himself at risk, both physically and mentally. *Manhunter* is a thriller of the highest order, but in all honesty it can be somewhat disturbing at times. To catch a serial killer, William Petersen has to think like one, and that's a pretty terrifying proposition, don't you think? To think bad thoughts. You get them, don't you? Everybody does. We do. The key is not to be afraid. Embrace them. They are yours, after all. Thoughts, just thoughts. You haven't done anything wrong. At least, not yet. Let them wash over you and begone. It's simple, harmless fantasy. Everybody fantasizes, right? Sure they do. Everything's going to be OK. We promise.

Pop in the tape. Now sit on the couch. Are your feet up? Good. Now just relax. Dr. Lecter has a special prescription to ease your mind. And don't forget to check under the pillow before you go to sleep tonight. The Tooth Fairy left you a little present. A little token of his affection . . . just for you.

1986 (119 min.). William Petersen, Dennis Farina, Brian Cox, Tom Noonan. Dir.: Michael Mann.

    VS

Midnight Run 🌿 🌿 🌿 🌿

Ex-cop must get annoying fugitive from New York to Los Angeles.

There was a time when costarring with a dog was cool. You got together, you hashed out the script, no one pissed in the trailer and demanded watermelon juice. Old Yeller, Cujo, Toto—these dogs were professionals. Now you get *K-9* with James Belushi. Two *Beethoven* movies with Charles Grodin and that goddamn St. Bernard.

Grodin has his good days, though, and this is one of 'em. Bounty hunter De Niro must bring in ex-Mafia accountant on the run. But it ain't easy; Grodin doesn't fly.

Like many accountants, Charles carries the handy *Baked Potatoes Air Travel Translator* (Dell, $7.95), and he's not feeling good about this flight. You can tell from the first cockpit syllable if you're in for a competent cruise. If the word "folks" is involved and the guy sounds like he's in bed in Georgia watching TV with his wife, you're safe. If he's coughing a lot, giggling, or accidentally leaves the mike open and is reading *Baked Potatoes* reviews to a cackling cadre of copilots, it is not good.

Commit these other handy translations to memory:

"It may be a little turbulent today" = "You will soon be screaming and vomiting"

"We'll be serving our complimentary light lunch" = "A seven-grain roll is more than enough for your starving, helpless body"

"Our captain has informed us of a slight technical problem" = "You are dead"

1988 (122 min.). Robert De Niro, Charles Grodin, Yaphet Kotto. Dir.: Martin Brest.

VS

Miller's Crossing 🌿 🌿 🌿 🌿

Double- and triple-crossing in the mythical gangland universe of Joel and Ethan Coen.

The most underappreciated film in the Coen brothers' pantheon of classics. It gets swept under the carpet by those who can quote *Raising*

Arizona verbatim, or the film-school fanatics who dissect *Blood Simple* and *Barton Fink* shot by shot. But here's a vote for *Miller's Crossing* as the best of the lot. It's like a beautiful painting: The colors and broad strokes are nice, but it's the small details that matter. It's the only movie on the Coens' résumé in which the Coens themselves aren't the story. The story's the story, and despite how much we love to watch great directors direct, isn't that how it should be? The Coens are so prevalent in every scene that you never notice them. Every moment is finely crafted and confidently displayed. It's a good, good thing. It's two hours of that moment you first become aware of how baked you are and you just can't help but smile, baby. All of their movies are winners, but this one's a champion. Watch it, and be a champion too.

1990 (115 min.). Gabriel Byrne, Albert Finney, Marcia Gay Harden, John Turturro, Jon Polito. Dir.: Joel Coen.

👁 🦅 ⅃ VS

A Nightmare on Elm Street (the first one)

Pre—benzoil peroxide monster terrorizes dreamworld of helpless, death-bound teens.

You'd think after five nightmares on Elm Street, people would stop moving there. "Oh, honey, isn't that the street where all those people keep getting killed? I heard it's a drug-free community. Let's move there." Big deal, there's a guy with bad complexion and a knife-gloved hand. Just because he's face-challenged doesn't mean he's a criminal. Look at Geraldo.

Who needs teenagers anyway? All they do is get baked and watch TV. Rather have a Freddy Krueger in the neighborhood any day. He picks up after his dog, shovels his walk promptly, always brings a nice dish to the block party. Last year he brought those delicious brownies that made Uncle Bud shave his eyebrows off.

Sure, he infiltrates the dreams of local youths, often resulting in death. But it's worth it.

1984 (92 min.). John Saxon, Heather Langenkamp, Ronee Blakley, Robert Englund, Johnny Depp. Dir.: Wes Craven.

  vs

One Flew Over the Cuckoo's Nest 🌿 🌿 🌿 🌿

Adaptation of Ken Kesey novel featuring your friends from high school.

This tab has its ups and downs. Its ups are Jack Nicholson, Ken Kesey; it's the American Film Institute's sixth best American film ever made. Its downs are fugue, schizophrenia, deformity, and Nurse Ratched. You can't help thinking about that perfectly normal Harvard kid who started hearing aliens speak to him one day and hasn't left the Bellevue spaceship since. Totally random and a true story. He wakes up one day and bang. Thinking about hearing aliens is not what you want to be thinking about during Baked Potato viewing. That's OK, you're not hearing aliens. Probably. If only that fly would get off the screen and go out the window it'd be OK. It's a big window and it's wide open but the fly still keeps hitting the frame and bouncing back to the screen. Is that a piece of hair on the screen, or is it the tape? You ask your friend Kent but he's itching and scratching all over, claiming his body is infested with mites, and then he goes to take a shower and everyone else has left the room and you're stuck with Nurse Ratched, which is normally tolerable but now for some reason sounds like the devil playing a fiddle and screeching chalk on a blackboard and you shut it off but you can still see your reflection in the TV and it's all messed up and you start thinking of Rocky Dennis and your head is contorting like his and you're a total freak and suddenly, without warning, the whole visual field shatters like glass, falling away into a giant white screen where John Denver is sitting on a wooden chair playing a sitar and Brooke Shields is dancing the hopping-on-one-foot *Deliverance* dance in Indian dresses and your heart rate is rising and you blink again and you're in Robert Cormier's *I Am the Cheese* and all these giant faces are flipping you and finally, out of nowhere, someone taps you on the shoulder.

"Dude, put the movie in."

1975 (133 min.). Jack Nicholson, Brad Dourif, Louise Fletcher. Dir.: Milos Forman.

             VS

Planet of the Apes 🌿 🌿 🌿 🌿

All five movies.

So you think *Pulp Fiction* had a crazy time structure? Child's play. This series of films defined the term cyclical. Goes a little somethin' like this . . .

An astronaut named Taylor landed on the postapocalyptic earth of the future ruled by intelligent apes who subjugated humankind until Taylor's buddy Brent showed up and initiated a chain of events that led to a doomsday device being triggered in the Forbidden Zone destroying the planet but not before chimps Zira, Cornelius, and Dr. Somebody left the planet in Brent's spaceship traveling back in time to the early seventies where they were unfortunately murdered by the evil human military but not before they exchanged baby Milo with a circus chimp leaving Milo to be raised by kindly rube Ricardo Montalban and to grow up to be another ape played by Roddy McDowall who trained his simian brethren to revolt against their human rulers causing a nuclear war that devastated the planet leaving only apes and some mutated humans to fight for supremacy forcing Roddy to once again assume his hairy alter ego and rally his comrades to "Fight like apes!" and gain domination of the planet until Charlie Heston dropped in to start the whole ball of wax rolling again in an endless circle that could drive you crazy if you think about it too much and if you really want to know why turn to Appendix VI to be sure . . .

Planet of the Apes: *1968 (112 min.). Charlton Heston, Roddy McDowall, Kim Hunter, James Whitmore. Dir.: Franklin J. Schaffner.*

Beneath the Planet of the Apes: *1970 (95 min.). Heston, Hunter, James Franciscus. Dir.: Ted Post.*

Escape from the Planet of the Apes: *1971 (98 min.). McDowall, Hunter, Bradford Dillman, Sal Mineo, Ricardo Montalban. Dir.: Don Taylor.*

Conquest of the Planet of the Apes: *1972 (87 min.). McDowall, Don Murray, Montalban. Dir.: J. Lee Thompson.*

Battle for the Planet of the Apes: *1973 (92 min.). McDowall, Paul Williams, Claude Akins, John Huston. Dir.: J. Lee Thompson.*

   D   VL

Poltergeist 🍁 🍁 🍁 🍁

Real-estate tiff between dead people under a house and family in the house.

Backdraft taught us to buy First Alert smoke detectors and always attend the annual pancake breakfast. *Schindler's List* taught us that pot and the Holocaust don't always mix. *Poltergeist,* too, teaches us an important lesson: Don't build your house on a fucking graveyard.

You're in the big-chain video store with shwag selection. Ten raving, bug-eyed maniacs are waiting for you to come home with the call. You're browsing. The person next to you has seven tapes and Siamese twins, joined at the head, in a stroller. You can't find anything. The manager starts whispering into a walkie-talkie and presses a red button under the counter. Squads of riot police flood into the store. Total panic.

Just calm down. *Poltergeist* is one of the BPAC's "red alert" picks: It's safe and solid. You're guaranteed to have a good time watching it and so is everyone back at the ranch. So what if you've seen it a hundred times? Everyone has. You could've watched it this morning and it'll be just as good tonight. You won't be scared anymore, but you can remember what it was like and enjoy each classic moment like it was yesterday. Which it probably was. No one's ever disappointed when they hear "Hey, *Poltergeist* is on . . ." No one will be tonight.

Try not to remember what happened to the two daughters in real life.

Cowritten by Steven Spielberg.

1982 (114 min.). JoBeth Williams, Craig T. Nelson, Beatrice Straight. Dir.: Tobe Hooper.

VS

Predator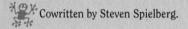

Arnold kicks ass in jungle.

We write Roger Ebert a message, feigning an appreciation for his screenwriting effort, *Beyond the Valley of the Dolls,* all in an attempt to get a simple guest-review from the man. And what does he say? "I think your book is wrongheaded," and, "Why would you want to dull your sensibilities by smoking pot?" Dull our sensibilities by smoking pot?

Before *Baked Potatoes* you had to endure people like that, people who actually have the gall to use the word *wrongheaded* in everyday conversation.

Well, that was then. This is *Predator.* Hard-hitting, skin-tearing, blood-wrenching, all-out madness. Go down the checklist:

Good kills: ____
Big guns: ____
Pointless female character: ____
Bad-ass villain: ____
Jesse "The Body" Ventura: ____
Quality one-liners: ____
Deforestation: ____
Sonny Landham: ____

Wrongheaded? Try again.

> We apologize for not killing Shane Black somewhere in this review.

1987 (107 min.). Arnold Schwarzenegger, Carl Weathers, Elpidia Carrillo. Dir.: John McTiernan.

The Princess Bride 🌿 🌿 🌿

Dong, Grandpa is speaking to you.

Like many children's films, *The Princess Bride* falls into that ever-growing coincidence of being especially good high. Kids are smoking pot again these days and, well, it shows. Certainly makes all the difference at assemblies.

Whether you're eight or eighty there's something alluring about the fantasy, the magic, the unforgettable battle between two master swordsmen. It reminds one of that *Knight Rider* episode where you learned about Zeno's Paradox: What happens when an unstoppable force meets an indestructible object. You were little then, but now you know: It results in David Hasselhoff.

But let's not get into David Hasselhoff; that's a book within itself. *Buzz Hasselhoff: Someone Please Help.*

Today it's *Princess Bride:* A boy's grandfather reads him a charming storybook tale. Light but fulfilling. Happy. Clever. Well-told, well-acted, solid.

1987 (98 min.). Cary Elwes, Mandy Patinkin, Robin Wright, Wallace Shawn, Peter Falk, Andre the Giant, Chris Sarandon, Christopher Guest, Billy Crystal, Carol Kane, Fred Savage, Peter Cook, Mel Smith. Dir.: Rob Reiner.

 vs

Pulp Fiction

Amorous picnic turned Chinese-star melee between pack of Regular and Homestyle citrus-juice drinkers.

Tarantino can't stop moving. He can't stop gesticulating. He can't stop dropping the bombs. Classic line after classic scene, it's like Pearl Harbor all over again.

But today we live in peace, multicultural neighbors in one big, happy melting pot, or salad bowl, to be more precise. You see, the salad bowl allows all the different vegetables to retain their uniqueness while still being a single salad. The melting pot insists upon the decomposition of all elements into one ugly brown mass.

Pulp Fiction is a 100 percent salad. John Travolta, fully hydrated and tossed with Samuel Jackson as hard-crunching iceberg gangsters with taste. An unexpected but not unpleasant slice of Bruce Willis. A garnish of Christopher Walken. No bad eggs, and a leafy Eric Stoltz, compulsory drug addict, a clear nod to the fold.

Whether you're Italian, French, or just honey mustard, this one's worth undressing. If you haven't seen it, if you're afraid it's too violent, save it for the queen, and suck it up. Everyone needs their ruffage.

All the clocks in the film are set to 4:20.

1994 (153 min.). John Travolta, Samuel L. Jackson, Uma Thurman, Harvey Keitel, Tim Roth, Amanda Plummer, Maria de Medeiros, Ving Rhames, Eric Stoltz, Rosanna Arquette, Christopher Walken, Bruce Willis. Dir.: Quentin Tarantino.

Real Genius 🌿 🌿 🌿

Baked Potatoes save world.

There's a category lurking out there that we're all aware of but rarely discuss. It's been repressed in the movie-watching consciousness. It's not the homeless. It's not racism. It's not the thing about Richard Gere and the gerbil.

It's the Cable Classics. The *Eddie and the Cruisers* of the world. The *Iron Eagle*s, the *Gotcha!*s. Every now and then one of them breaks out of the genre, smashing free of the neutral zone and establishing itself as a legitimate life form.

Real Genius is one of the chosen. Jim Morrison, before he remembered he was Val Kilmer, stars in tale of hot-shot kid Einsteins whose laser creation is co-opted by evil artisans of Defense Department. You gotta wonder. Why is it that Army people are generally such assholes? Why is it that everyone who's supposed to be protecting you always wants to kick your ass? Ever notice that?

Real Genius: just what the title promises, even though it might've been an accident.

Look out for baked guy in basement and giant Jiffy Pop monster that demolishes a house.

1985 (104 min.). Val Kilmer, Gabe Jarret, Jonathan Gries, Michelle Meyrink, William Atherton, Patti D'Arbanville, Severn Darden. Dir.: Martha Coolidge.

Reefer Madness 🌿 🌿 🌿

**American teens of 1930s have personality and genetic
hemorrhaging, grow unexplained vestigial limbs, commence
fit of wilding under influence of cannabis.**

Considered shocking in it's day, the 1936 potnophobic propaganda
piece originally titled *Tell Your Children* depicts, in sixty-seven legendary
and comically absurd minutes, a complete descent from respectable
American adolescence to raving insanity and murder. All from the evil
"marihuana." With an *h*.

The sad part? It could have been written yesterday.

The intro says it all:

> The motion picture you are about to witness may startle you. It would
> not have been possible otherwise to sufficiently emphasize the fright-
> ful toll of the new drug menace which is destroying the youth of Amer-
> ica in alarmingly increasing numbers.
>
> Marihuana is that drug—a violent narcotic—an unspeakable
> scourge—*the real Public Enemy Number One!*
>
> Its first effect is sudden, violent, uncontrollable laughter; then
> come dangerous hallucinations—space expands, time slows down, al-
> most stands still . . . fixed ideas come next, conjuring up monstrous ex-
> travagances, followed by emotional disturbances, the total inability to
> direct thoughts, the loss of all power to resist physical emotions . . .
> leading finally to acts of shocking violence . . . ending often in incur-
> able insanity.
>
> In picturing its soul-destroying effects no attempt was made
> to equivocate. The scenes and incidents, while fictionalized for
> the purposes of this story, are based upon actual research into the re-
> sults of marihuana addiction. If their stark reality will make you
> *think,* will make you aware that something *must be done* to wipe out
> this ghastly menace, then the picture will not have failed in its pur-
> pose . . .
>
> Because the dread *marihuana* may be reaching forth next for your
> son or daughter . . . or yours . . . or *Yours!*"

Too late.

1936 (67 min.). Dave O'Brien, Dorothy Short, Warren McCollum. Dir.: Louis Gasnier.

VL

Repo Man 🍁 🍁 🍁 🍁

Mom, I had to repossess Uncle Bud's car and I found a dead llama in the trunk.

Baked Potatoes sometimes hold "odd" jobs. Sanitary engineer, chopped-meat sculptor, assistant to the petroleum consultant. We don't need these types of jobs; we take them by choice, to stay in touch with the common man, to observe the absurdity of the general public in action.

Now, there's a big difference between observing the general public and actually coming in contact with them. Being a repo man is a touch over the line.

As is Emilio Estevez. He can't even see the line anymore. Jesus, you almost feel bad for Emilio Estevez. Tragic. Anyway, that's life, and Emilio indoctrinated into the art of car repossession by the always-dependable Harry Dean Stanton.

If you're in the mood to give society (including punks themselves) the finger, roast up and prepare for a seriously strange trip in a Chevy Malibu.

Violent, ruthless black-comedy homage to the punk aesthetic.

1984 (92 min.). Emilio Estevez, Harry Dean Stanton, Sy Richardson. Dir.: Alex Cox.

  ♪ VS

Reservoir Dogs 🌿 🌿 🌿 🌿

Bank heist gone bad.

Seen it already? Then you know what you're in for. Sit back and relish the emergence of a Baked Potato giving other Baked Potatoes something to get baked about.

Haven't seen it yet? Grab some jabooby and don't be concerned if the heist confuses for the first twenty minutes. That's the beauty of it. Figuring out Tarantino's story line is like gathering up the remains of your most recent multichemical blackout. Bits and pieces come back with time, order in but particular no. Be patient. Everything will be explained.

To those in the company of sensitive viewers, duct-tape them to lounge chairs and staple their eyelids to their foreheads. Some people don't know what's good for them, so tonight, you do the thinking.

Theaters with brains show *Reservoir Dogs* as a midnight special. Go for the big screen and smoke in your seat. No one really cares.

1992 (99 min.). Harvey Keitel, Tim Roth, Michael Madsen, Steve Buscemi, Chris Penn, Lawrence Tierney. Dir.: Quentin Tarantino.

  VS

Richard Pryor— Live in Concert 🌿 🌿 🌿 🌿

The king of stand-up at the top of his game.

We're not saying that you have to be on drugs to be funny, but you do have to wonder sometimes. Just look at the early cast of the Not Ready for Prime Time Players. Wasted, they delivered us *Animal House, The Blues Brothers, Caddyshack, Meatballs,* and some of the greatest television ever to subvert the airwaves. Sober, they gave us *What About Bob?*, *The Great Outdoors*, *The Stuff*, *Caddyshack II*, *Cops and Robbersons*, and TV like *Kate & Allie.* You make the call.

The same goes for Richard Pryor. Straightened up, he barely tickled our fancy with *The Toy* and *Superman III.* But back in the day, when he was jacked up on Central America's finest cocaine and talked about it on-stage, well, you have to see it to believe it. The man knows no equal. Too bold a statement? Watch any Eddie Murphy tape and see how much of Pryor's style he copped. Throw on *Raw,* and Eddie will tell you the very same thing himself.

Unquestionably, the greatest stand-up comic of our time in his best video performance.

1979 (78 min.). Richard Pryor. Dir.: Jeff Margolis.

 F V$

Risky Business

What didn't happen when your parents went away.

Joel wants to go to college. Can you blame him? Where else is incessant pot smoking not only accepted but revered?

Activism is dead on campuses everywhere, but there's a good reason for it. It's been replaced by the full-time vocation of Baked Potato mastery. Let's revamp the curriculum: Baked Potatoes 101: General Etiquette and Lawbreaking. Baked Potatoes 102: Buying—Shades of Green, Bag-Size Deception, Basic Fractions. Baked Potatoes 206: Jonesing—Coping with Addiction, Desperation, Resin. Baked Potatoes 403 (Graduate Seminar): The Business of Pot—Hydroponics, Where to Buy a DEA Uniform, Air, Land, and Sea Smuggling. Guest lecturer: Robert Parish. All pass/fail. All papers.

Now that's a course load you can believe in.

And don't forget the required texts: ten copies *Baked Potatoes,* three copies *Voices of the Xiled,* and *Risky Business.* Don't sweat it, you've got the Cliffs Notes: Tom Cruise, parents go away, prostitutes and teenagers, Rebecca De Mornay, glass eggs, dancing in underwear, Ray·Bans.

A solid 3.8, high honors.

1983 (96 min.). Tom Cruise, Rebecca De Mornay, Curtis Armstrong. Dir.: Paul Brickman.

 VS

The Road Warrior

Mel Gibson returns to yet another postapocalyptic nightmare world where oil is the most precious commodity.

It was four in the morning and we were high as bats, watching the tenth movie from the list of absolute "must-sees" that somebody's boss faxed us. And this one was just a little bit worse than the other nine utterly unbearable pieces of shit. We have to admit, we were getting a little bitter at the guy. Our anger might've been enhanced by the fact that the boss was just another ex-hippie who'd sold out for the Range Rover and the security of the corporate infrastructure. In the heat of the moment, it's difficult to say. We loaded the car up with rope, shotgun shells, and turpentine, determined to exact our vengeance. All we needed now was something to fire us up to commit this random yet completely justifiable act of violence. Reaching into a dusty box of old videotapes, we found the one man who could give us the inspiration we craved. His name?

Mad Max. *The Road Warrior.* It took us thirty seconds to realize that the years have not diluted this film's impact one iota. Nothing can prepare you for the mind-bending stunts and raw bloodshed, or the characters that barely have time to speak before they're run over by a truck or lit on fire. And the relentless pace of the final chase is unmatched in film history. *The Road Warrior* is as reliable as a Far Side collection next to the toilet bowl, and just as user-friendly. Yes, you've seen it seventy-three times, but you've smoked pot on more nights than that, and you haven't stopped do-ing that, right? Do yourself a favor. Spark up number seventy-four.

1981 (94 min.). Mel Gibson, Bruce Spence, Vernon Wells, Emil Minty, Kjell Nilsson. Dir.: George Miller.

♪   VS

Saturday Night Fever

When I dance, why do I look like a pregnant cow?

There was a time when life was all about the classics. *The Love Boat, Mission: Impossible, Starsky and Hutch.* A time when an honest cat could wear a turtleneck. When a bicentennial quarter meant something to a kid. For God's sake, Billy Joel sounded decent. Almost.

Now all you get is tummysizing and John Davidson in a Hawaiian shirt. That's what it's come to. The star of *That's Incredible!* relegated to late-night info-hell.

There was a time when Baked Potatoes roamed the fields with pride, numerous and majestic like the great caribou. A time where potnocen-trism was not about separatism. Only now are we rising like the phoenix from our basements and ghettos and venturing again into the light.

Things were different in the seventies, and films were one of those things. *Saturday Night Fever?* Enough said. The disco, the lapels, John Travolta, and that well-placed one-hitter of *The Nanny,* Fran Drescher. The whole decade was stoned—the filmmakers, the actors, the govern-ment. And hence the work endures.

1977 (119 min.). John Travolta, Karen Lynn Gorney, Barry Miller, Donna Pescow. Dir.: John Badham.

      VS

sex, lies, and videotape

Baked Potato visits old college bud, snakes his wife.

James Spader carries one key. Lives out of his car. Into kinky video-tapes. That's a hero we like to see. Steven Soderbergh deserves an award. Sure he got that Behind the Palme d'or thing, but what does that mean?

We're talking about the latest gemola in Tinseltown. The thing the Scientologists are mad over. The treasure that Spielberg's been bucking for. BP Development in conjunction with BP Merchandising in conjunction with the Baked Potato General are proud to announce the Hash Brown, just like the Oscar but with long hair, stockier, and made entirely of potato and tofutti. An awards event that rewards true baked merit, an event to honor and praise the Baked Potato films of the year.

And Soderbergh is certainly worthy.

Five characters, five locations, low-budget indie bombshell, *sex, lies* is generally credited as one of the first crossover "art" films to spank the modern mainstream. People have sex, people betray each other, people fall in love. The usual human slop-fest but extremely well-drooled.

1989 (100 min.). James Spader, Andie MacDowell, Peter Gallagher, Laura San Giacomo. Dir.: Steven Soderbergh.

        VS

The Shining

Excuse me young man, is this the kosher dining room?

Bring your bag and bring your brain, for at the Overlook Hotel you'll find an elevator filled with blood and *murder* spelled backward, but they don't take American Express.

No matter which way you cut it, you've got problems. AmEx gives you service, but you've got an annual fee. Visa, you owe a hundred dollars' interest by the time you get through to complain. Discover—it has something to do with Sears. Which makes one nervous.

Say what you will about Jack Nicholson; he does justice to *The Shining*. Say what you will about Stephen King and Stanley Kubrick; they have their moments. Quite a few, in fact. And the kicker is Shelley Duvall, superior work as the estranged wife of writer-gone-mad Nicholson.

Critics gave *The Shining* mixed reviews, but they weren't stoned. By the way, if you notice the neighborhood kids wandering the streets at night chanting *seotatop dekab* and carrying large kitchen knives, don't worry. It's resin from the conversion to metric.

1980 (142 min.). Jack Nicholson, Shelley Duvall, Scatman Crothers, Danny Lloyd. Dir.: Stanley Kubrick.

Sixteen Candles

The first intelligent teen comedy.

Picture this scene: A fourteen-year-old boy and girl sit together at a lonely table in the school cafeteria. They pop their zits, finish some senior's homework, and stare longingly at the couple who occupies the center table: the popular, ruggedly handsome captain of the football team and his girlfriend, the spectacularly beautiful and well-endowed queen of the cheerleaders.

In real life, the outcast boy goes to a bathroom stall and maniacally masturbates to thoughts of holding the cheerleader's naked body in his arms, making love to her . . . well. So well, in fact, that fourteen to fifteen of the cheerleader's even more beautiful best friends, who look just like the women in his favorite porno mag, want to have sex with him simultaneously.

The girl, wracked with embarrassment and self-doubt over her appearance and the fact that no one notices her, stares dreamily at the BMOC. She imagines that he's not a self-absorbed, meatheaded bully. He's actually a shy, sensitive, tender Romeo who's sick of his airheaded, bubble-breasted girlfriend. He'd rather have a romantic, candlelit dinner alone with our heroine instead of getting wasted and vomiting all over the fifty-yard line with his buddies.

In *Sixteen Candles,* the fantasies come true. Score one for us dorks in the corner.

1984 (93 min.). Molly Ringwald, Anthony Michael Hall, Justin Henry, John Cusack, Joan Cusack. Dir.: John Hughes.

   vs

Slacker 🌿 🌿 🌿 🌿

Follow the lives of the disaffected and disenchanted youth of Austin, Texas.

Go to any café at any college or Seattleized town in America and listen to your fellow patrons. As if you had the choice. Listen to the pontification. Listen to those who KNOW they know what is right. What is true. Listen to the political posturing by the army of pseudointellectuals and those who seek the argumentative victory by out-shouting their opponents. Listen to the references picked up between crossword puzzles and placed skillfully in conversations about gun control, free trade, and the legalization of controlled substances. Listen to the sound of your teeth grinding in frustration. It's hard to listen to anything in particular because they just won't stop babbling like so many sparrows in a tree! To make matters worse, the sparrows are far more interesting. Only one thing to do. Stand up. Put on your favorite Cliff Clavin suit, grab the submachine gun you have a constitutional right to bear, and offer them a choice. Shut up, or . . .

Better rent *Slacker* instead. Pacify yourself in more ways than one.

Rick Linklater has brilliantly transmogrified the mindless chatter into something worth watching. He turns a skillful comic eye toward every closet Tarantino, unrewarded genius, and couch-bound stoner and never makes us . . . er, them look bad. They actually look like people you might like to meet. And if by chance they get on your nerves, you can always stop the tape, instead of pulling out the Uzi and taking a bite from the Charles Whitman sandwich that the real world seems to offer.

1991 (97 min.). Nobody you've ever heard of. Dir.: Richard Linklater.

 𝔇 𝒱𝓛

Something Wild 🌿 🌿 🌿 🌿

Repressed corporate tool with potential hooks up with cool, freewheeling, whacked-out psycho chick.

People in the know say Chris Evert's the bitch and Martina's cool. We can see through America's love affair with Chrissy. It's because she's "pretty" and Martina's a brute. Well, BP Intelligence reports that Chris was slapping Jimmy Connors around and that's why he left her and that's why he's sleeping with Dick Enberg now.

It all started with Ray Liotta. He looks so damn evil on the outside, but underneath he's probably fairly evil. Ray shows up to ace mild-mannered businessman Jeff "Charlie" Daniels, who's on the inside-out forehand of his life, taken in by the volleys of wacky, flighty, sexy Melanie Griffith. Just a cyclopean blip in the theaters, totally underloved and disadvantaged, *Something Wild* is like a topspin lob. Unpredictable, bold. You're just sitting at the net like the let-court judge wondering why you never saw it coming.

Before it bounces—quick!—pull the Yannick Noah between-the-legs return and smoke a bowl with Johnny Mac. He's just doin' a little commentary with Pat Summerall, who's slowly mutating into a fish.

Unsung hero that qualifies for the Open. Absolutely worth the deuce.

1986 (113 min.). Jeff Daniels, Melanie Griffith, Ray Liotta. Dir.: Jonathan Demme.

♪   vs

Star Trek II: The Wrath of Khan 🌿 🌿 🌿

Ricardo Montalban vs. William "Bug Out" Shatner in battle of demented ego-freakers.

Captain Kirk was a hero, Oprah was in a thin phase, Flintstones Vitamins, mom's quaaludes, model-airplane glue, stabbing other kids with pencils . . . the good old days.

Then you grow up and it crumbles. Both your parents had sex changes but dressed like each other so you never knew. William Shatner's bald. Sulu bonked Uhura. A Vulcan's narrating Discovery Channel segments.

Then the big one: Khan is Mr. Roarke. Oh, that hurts. You just know that Herve Villechaize is bungling through the hallways accosting female officers or hiding somewhere in engineering. Maybe he's not dead. Maybe he transported himself into your kitchen where he's now preparing to burst out naked and flit about the room like a headless chicken.

There's only one way to snap him out of it: *The Wrath of Khan.* Based on the 1967 "Space Seed" episode, Kirk and crew commence an entrancing battle with master Khan, the commendably able villain out for revenge. Kirk's former lover is introduced, as is Spock's previously unknown son, and his own eventual death.

Herve's hooked. You've grabbed his attention and diffused the scene, transposing the evening from a minor bout with chaos to a rather agreeable Baked Potato soiree. Well done.

1982 (113 min.). William Shatner, Leonard Nimoy, Ricardo Montalban, DeForest Kelley, Nichelle Nichols, James Doohan, George Takei, Walter Koenig. Dir.: Nicholas Meyer.

VS

Star Wars 🌿 🌿 🌿 🌿 🌿

If you don't know the plot to Star Wars, please bludgeon yourself to death.

When you were young there were only two things you wanted. To be a Jedi Master and to have the power to stop time and wreak havoc on your sixth-grade classmates, frozen and impotent, as you wild through the halls hurling Apple II Pluses at cafeteria aides.

Harrison Ford made it out alive. Carrie Fisher does OK. But what happened to Luke? Did he go back to the Dagoba system for more training?

Petty jabs aside, this may be the only film in the last twenty-five years whose first viewing approximates the first time you got stoned. Not the first time you smoked pot, but the first time you didn't have to fake being high. The moment that changed your life forever and landed you in this book.

No film has ever come close to the sense of sheer wonder that George Lucas's work of genius provides. You can't take it with you, but every now and then the feeling can almost be reclaimed. Almost.

1977 (121 min.). Mark Hamill, Carrie Fisher, Harrison Ford, Alec Guinness. Dir.: George Lucas.

VS

Strange Brew 🌿 🌿 🌿

SCTV's Doug and Bob McKenzie vs. scum-hound brewmeister in steel-cage death match over case of beer.

Everyone knows a Baked Potato who is in the midst of concocting a "home brew." All you hear for weeks is about how Franklin's "home brew" is almost ready. Everyone goes over to his house on the big day and drinks the stuff. Sure, it's the most hideous liquid ever fermented, sure, it has "pulp" the size of bouillon cubes, but everyone pretends to love it. "Yeah, man, it's really full-bodied." "Yeah, I agree, it's got a real barley tinge to it." "Yeah, man, I have a cube of hops in my throat and my brain is suffocating."

It's great how the world operates. You go to a girl's house and she pulls out a bag of hay from a farm and hands it to you and says, "Hey, man, check out the kind buds," and of course you don't want to offend, so you're like, "Yeah, it's that yellow hybrid from Prague, wow, couldn't even ask for a bowl."

Imagine how fast an honest person would be killed in this world. "Hey, Franklin, the home brew's like sewage, man. Good job." "Yeah, you're showing me hay here, you know what I'm saying, like hay from a farm." It's not popular to tell the truth; that's why no one does it.

Strange Brew, on the other hand, is a lager you can trust. It's certifiably moronic but all the more refreshing and reliable. After all is said and done, the human struggle always filters down to substance abuse. Your faith in humanity is restored.

1983 (90 min.). Rick Moranis, Dave Thomas, Max von Sydow. Dir.: Rick Moranis, Dave Thomas.

       VS

The Terminator 🌿 🌿 🌿

Arnold comes back from future, kicks ass.

When you rent *The Terminator* don't sit near the door. Sit in that green cushion chair that cost five dollars and everyone fights over. So it's infested with microorganisms. Big deal. Remember the days when spotting a rotifer was better than watching wars on TV? Anchor yourself, sweetheart, 'cause this one'll blow you right out of that pit you call home. Arnie's got firepower. More muscle than a phase plasma rifle.

Nice night for a walk? Not so fast. Better drive, it's cold. And not to Blockbuster, please. They rape you and support an antipot agenda. Let's get serious about who we give our business to. Don't you think it's about time for a bumper sticker? I'M STONED AND CAN'T SEE THE ROAD. Kind of long but it's better than VISUALIZE WHIRLED PEAS or NORTHERN BY BIRTH. SOUTHERN BY THE GRACE OF GOD. Plus, the fine men and women of law enforcement will really respect your honesty and not pull you over.

Indestructible monster returns from future to kill enemy's mother who's Linda Hamilton? Sounds like cheese? It's not. It's a classic. *The Terminator.*

1984 (108 min.). Arnold Schwarzenegger, Michael Biehn, Linda Hamilton, Paul Winfield, Lance Henriksen, Bill Paxton. Dir.: James Cameron.

J   VS

....

Terminator 2: Judgment Day 🌿 🌿 🌿 🌿

Arnold comes back from future, kicks ass again.

T2 delivers on all the necessary Arnold fronts: mind-numbing action, special effects, and the requisite one-liners. Most of the time you don't even notice the absurdity of the liquid-metal terminator's decision to "sneak up" on the Connor family in a police uniform, with a face that never changes. It's Arnie, so we try not to think too hard about it.

But there is one problem that just keeps irritating us. It was established in both films that the artificial intelligence behind the terminators was invented by the mighty Cyberdyne Corporation. To accomplish this feat, they used technology left behind by the machine that Sarah defeated in the first movie. It was also established in *T2* that Cyberdyne hadn't yet deciphered how said technology worked. So if the terminators from the second movie are destroyed in a vat of liquid metal, along with the memory chip from the first movie, what did Cyberdyne use to invent the technology in the first place? Why else would our heroes bother to steal and melt the chip, unless it was to keep it from Cyberdyne? Armageddon, or "Judgment Day," would never have happened. John Connor would never have needed to send Kyle Reese back in time to save his mother. John would never even have been conceived. The first film should never have happened. The second film should never have happened. This review should never have happened.

Please tear at perforation that was too expensive to print and is instead suggested by a dotted line and discard.

1991 (136 min.). Arnold Schwarzenegger, Linda Hamilton, Edward Furlong, Robert Patrick. Dir.: James Cameron.

VS

. . . .

They Live ❦ ❦ ❦

It's not our fault that society is crumbling. It's actually a race of aliens masquerading as humans that bombards us with subliminal messages telling us to keep our minds asleep.

So what if the ending sucked, à la every John Car**P**enter film since the days **O**f Snake Plissken and Doc Loomis? So wha**T I**f the producer**S** slapped on the bud**G**et clamps and g**O**t caught using **O**ne of the scanners from *Ghostbusters* in a pinch? (Look for the scene when the heroes hiDe from two guards in the tunnels. It's there.) So what? This movie makes the final cut for one reason and one reason alone. Its name is Rowdy Roddy Piper. Save up the resin ball and test yOur sTaying power for the eternal wrestlIng Sequence in the alley. The scouRge of the WWF shows off his entIre repertoire, from the suplex to a tasty sunset flip. It has to end, riGht? It'll be over soon . . . rigHt? RighT? They can't PoSsibly . . . ? Patience, Grasshopper. They can and they do. SoMetimes you have to just let it be and enjOy the ride. A waKe-and-bakE specIal served any way you wanT it. The Committee's breakfasT recommendation? TwO eggs over easy, a tall glass of TaNg, *They LIve,* and all The green stuff you can mustEr.

1988 (97 min.). Roddy Piper, Keith David, Meg Foster. Dir.: John Carpenter.

  VS

The Thing 🍁 🍁 🍁 🍁

An isolated team of researchers in the Arctic discovers that we're not all alone in the universe.

Have you ever looked in the mirror and not recognized the face? Yes, it looks familiar, but is that really you? Are you positive? And your voice . . . sometimes it just doesn't sound true. Like when you used to spell a word five different ways, and each way looked equally wrong and right. It causes you to wonder. Is that how other people hear you? You can write it off as déjà vu. Or maybe, just maybe, all those early morning sessions are starting to get to you. The defenses are coming down like so many walls of Jericho. There are two ways to go with this. The first involves doctors and experimental psychoactive medication. The other?

Could be you're not sick at all. Could be you're not *you* anymore. Not *really.* Who then? Watch *The Thing,* and get one possible interpretation. We don't mean the original "Attack of the Carrot Man," but John Carpenter's faithful and gory adaptation of John Campbell's short story

"Who Goes There?" Intense and scary enough to bring even the deepest identity crises to the surface. It's got a patient director at the top of his game, Kurt Russell when he had juice, BP superhero Keith David, and special effects that still get the job done over a decade later. Will it ease your troubled mind? Probably not. But even if you are an alien imitation of who you used to be, you can still get high and watch movies, right? Right. So what's the worry? Whoever you are, *The Thing* is the thing.

1982 (108 min.). Kurt Russell, Keith David, A. Wilford Brimley, Richard Dysart, Richard Masur. Dir.: John Carpenter.

    VS

Time Bandits

Honey, I shrunk the kids.

There's no way around it. *Time Bandits* has a lot of midgets in it. And if you've had bad experiences with the height challenged, well, it's gonna take some real maturity. Do it for Tattoo. Every day he bounded up that tall, difficult-to-negotiate bell tower and told you the plane was on its way. All those days on the set with Ricardo Montalban.

Time Bandits is its own fantasy, though, a wondrous film, a reliable source of the highest order. Little British kid hooks up with band of crooks who've stolen God's time-portal map and travel the ages in pillaging-looting romp. Something you can relate to? Afraid so. Costumes, carcasses filled with fruit, time travel, the *Titanic,* giant ogres, parents turned into black carbon pellets.

What else could a kid ask for?

1981 (110 min.). John Cleese, Sean Connery, Shelley Duvall, Katherine Helmond, Ian Holm. Dir.: Terry Gilliam.

   VS

Tremors

A small desert town is terrorized by carnivorous monsters.

So . . . what's the plot again? There are these giant, mutant worms that rise from underground to eat anybody they find on the surface? Cool.

1990 (96 min.). Kevin Bacon, Fred Ward, Finn Carter, Michael Gross, Reba McEntire. Dir.: Ron Underwood.

   ♂   VS

WarGames

Baked Potatoes save world.

Somehow you tend to file *WarGames* into that geeks-at-the-science-fair, eighties-shwag Dabney Coleman netherworld. The truth of the matter is quite different. The truth is that there's nothing wrong with being into science. Or even being a little weirder than everyone else. Now, having a big or deformed nose, that's a different story.

Experiencing the world high can be a wonderful thing. Food tastes better. Music sounds better. You're more effective as a bus driver or subway car operator.

The same goes for *WarGames:* high quality and not as fluffy as memory deceives. Dabney Coleman, more than hateable, and Matthew Broderick and Ally Sheedy, a really touching romance. The computer stuff completely works. Stephen Falken, the crazy creator . . . works. Hidden password . . . works. Nuclear war? Well, whatever. We used to be scared. *WarGames* draws you in and delivers the Hiroshima you might not expect.

 "I think we need to beef up security around the Whopper."

1983 (110 min.). Matthew Broderick, Ally Sheedy, Dabney Coleman,
John Wood. Dir.: John Badham.

  VS

The Warriors 🌿 🌿 🌿 🌿

Street gang battles back to home turf.

Ah, this one reminds you of middle school. When you were perse-
cuted as a stoner and had to keep seeing that guidance counselor with
the clubfoot.

The Warriors isn't about all that psychobabble. Therapy is for pussies,
anyway. This baby is up-front ass-kicking with a dash of creativity and a
dose of that seventies sort of cop-show medallion tripsterness that
seemed to permeate the decade.

Admit it. You did it, too. Alone in the basement. Out behind the
garbage dumpster. Back in the woods. When no one was around. Maybe
you still do it. All you need is a six-pack of Coke or a bag of returnables.
Skinny fingers help.

Clink. Clink. Clink.

Can you dig it?

That depends. If you can't appreciate a solid baseball-bat bludgeoning
or the annoying cadence of overused alliteration stand clear. In the
words of Luther: "Warriors, come out to play . . . eeee . . . yay."

1979 (90 min.). Michael Beck, James Remar, Deborah Van Valkenburgh.
Dir.: Walter Hill.

  VS

Weird Science 🌿 🌿 🌿

Computer-generated sexpot rescues geeks from social ill-repute.

Many of you have spent hours trying to get Kelly LeBrock naked and at your command. The trick is doing it in your mind instead of for real. There's no way her agent is sending her to your hacker basement-pit just because you're controlling NATO's nuclear arsenal.

Weird Science is the exception. A charming, generally unchallenging but legendary male-fantasy cable classic that speaks to those who've lost speech capability. If you find yourself crying on the phone to your mother and realize it's the MCI operator, it's time for a change of plans. Searching for that point where pi repeats can wait till morning. It's time for some mid-eighties Anthony Michael Hall titillation.

1985 (94 min.). Kelly LeBrock, Anthony Michael Hall, Ilan Mitchell-Smith, Robert Downey, Jr. Dir.: John Hughes.

 VS

Who'll Stop the Rain 🌿 🌿 🌿

A Vietnam veteran is forced to go on the run with a huge shipment of smuggled heroin.

It's the movie to watch when you feel the inescapable desire to indulge that jaded, cynical, depressed, self-righteous side of you. In a positive way. The cynicism dripping from this exploration of post-sixties disillusion should be allowed to coagulate at the bottom of the bowl, then scraped up and savored later in the evening, when you're feeling more up to it. It's an experience we all need at some time or another. If you're looking for some giggles or mindless action, stay away. But if that ride on the subway each morning is getting you down, or if the boss won't get off your ass, or if it just hit you that your bachelor's degree will better serve you as a post–bowel movement grooming tool, then take a shot at answering Creedence's question. You won't feel disappointed. You'll feel . . . justified.

1978 (126 min.). Nick Nolte, Tuesday Weld, Michael Moriarty, Ray Sharkey, Charles Haid, Richard Masur. Dir.: Karel Reisz.

 VS

Willy Wonka and the Chocolate Factory

Baked guy runs chocolate factory, surrounds self with midgets.

Willy Wonka is another one of those "children's" flicks, and we all know what that means. "Family values," "sacrifice," "an operator will be right with you." It's all code. Häagen-Dazs? Made in New Jersey. Samuel Adams? "Boston Beer Company, Boston Mass., PA." Boston Beer Company in Pennsylvania? You see, you can fool a human, but you can't fool a Baked Potato. Fry us, poke holes with a fork, mash away—these are but tiny jabs in our seasonal immortality. Poor player.

Now, *Willy Wonka* states its purpose and delivers. No fronts, no marketing, just classic all the way through. The everlasting gob stopper. Levitating soda. Lickable, fruit-flavored wallpaper. Little purple dudes who dance and sing. Charlie scores the last golden ticket and wins a tour of the mystical factory.

A psychedelic steamboat ride to nowhere on a chocolate river? Thought you'd never ask.

1971 (98 min.). Gene Wilder, Jack Albertson, Denise Nickerson, Peter Ostrum, Roy Kinnear, Aubrey Woods, Michael Bollner, Ursula Reit, Leonard Stone, Dodo Denney. Dir.: Mel Stuart.

 VS

The Wizard of Oz 🌿 🌿 🌿 🌿

A small-town girl opens the door to ... experience.

Here's what happened after we faded to black.

"...and then the people floating outside the window disappeared. The house stopped flying and spinning and landed with a loud crash. When I opened the door, the world wasn't black-and-white anymore ... it was in Technicolor. I was over the rainbow! There was a whole village of little people. They were called munchkins. And everybody sang and danced and they gave out lollipops and pretty flowers and there was this endless road made of yellow bricks. There were all sorts of wonderful creatures ... witches, flying monkeys, and a talking scarecrow ... and ... no, no I'm not lying ... Auntie Em, I swear, it's all true ... please, believe me, Auntie ... I didn't eat anything ... there were those poppies, but they only made me sleepy ... no ... please, don't ... I don't wanna go to The Clinic again! You just don't understand! I'm not like everyone else ... my mind's been opened! I can fly way up high! I can fly!"

"Henry. Call the doctors. Dorothy's been at the mushroom patch again."

1939 (101 min.). Judy Garland, Ray Bolger, Bert Lahr, Jack Haley, Frank Morgan, Margaret Hamilton. Dir.: Victor Fleming.

 VS

Any film directed by John Woo

Action films by Hong Kong's master of pyrotechnics.

Remember that field trip to the ballet back in second grade? You little girls out there watched with eyes wide and mouth agape at the beauty and delicacy of the dancers and their art. Ah, the music . . . the costumes . . . the choreography. A lifelong appreciation for dance probably began that day. And you little boys? Most of you were forced to sit by yourselves and be silent, separated for obscenely disruptive behavior involving a number of bodily functions. A lifelong fear of dance probably began that day.

There is little doubt that John Woo was one of these boys, but instead of running from the dance, he made it his own. He looked at the performance and realized that there was something missing, one vital element that would bring to the ballet a whole new audience demographic. Guns. Lots of them. Every kind imaginable. Preferably emptying their chambers into a flailing body or two. All his films have pretty good stories, but when you cut right to their essences, they each become the same. That's a good thing. John Woo gives us what he wanted to see as a child so many years ago.

Ballet . . . for little boys.

Especially see *A Better Tomorrow, I* and *II, Hard-Boiled,* and *The Killer.*

Forgive Woo for allowing himself to be Van Dammed in his first American picture. Everybody gets one mistake, right?

Woodstock 🍁 🍁 🍁 🍁

Woodstock.

There's an unwritten rule in the BPAC called the "if something cool happens don't try to reenact it twenty-five years later because you're a scumbag and have no life and want to milk it" rule. We've seen many a violation: the producers of *Kung Fu: The Legend Continues.* The Rolling Stones. And Woodstock II, another sham that scoffed the sequel clause and wound up like New Year's Eve: overpriced, nauseating, a complete letdown.

Skip the backlash over Greedstock '94. Forget the fact that every act that didn't OD within a year after the original Woodstock has embarrassed themselves by joining traveling-oldies shows. This documentary is one of a kind, largely because watching it is better than being there. As Chip Monck said, "It's easy to tell who was at Woodstock and who wasn't. Anyone who says it was great saw the movie." This could be you. The one drawback? The three-hour-plus running time. This easy-to-follow time chart will help you carry the day:

> Bowl #1: Just before Richie Havens
> Bowl #2: At Sha Na Na
> Bowl #3: Girl on mescaline
> Bowl #4–#6: Santana
> Bowl #7–#10: Hendrix
> Bowl #11: Static
> Bowl #12: Katie Couric

1970 (184 min.). Canned Heat, Richie Havens, The Who, Joan Baez, Country Joe and the Fish, Jimi Hendrix, Carlos Santana, Crosby, Stills, and Nash, The Jefferson Airplane, Joe Cocker, Sly and the Family Stone, John Sebastian, Arlo Guthrie, Ten Years After. Dir.: Michael Wadleigh.

Ð   VS

Yentl. 🌿 🌿 🌿 🌿 🌿

Just kidding.

1983 (134 min.). Barbra Streisand, Mandy Patinkin, Amy Irving. Dir.: Barbra Streisand.

VS

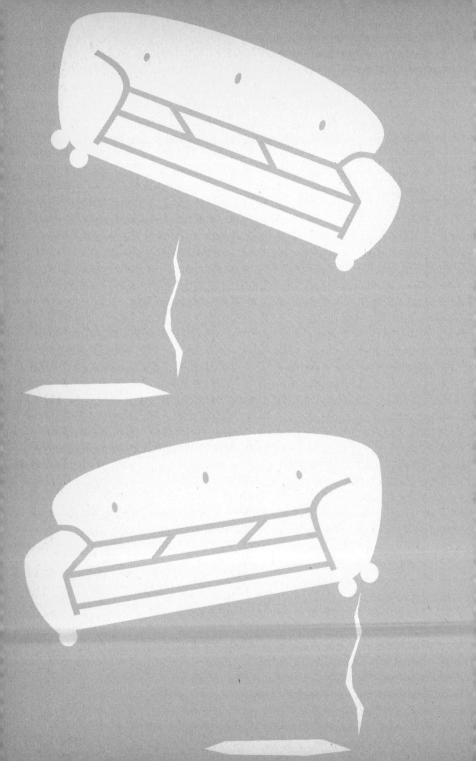

III.
Unsung Heroes

Looking for unsung heroes can be like searching for the promised land. Everyone tells you how to get there but their directions keep landing you in the desert. People lose faith and make pot calves.

When you find one, though, it's like manna. Seven-course meals that drop from the sky and hit you with the glory of hallelujah. They generally come in two types: (a) hidden gems you may have never seen before; and (b) films you're familiar with but wouldn't expect to deliver high.

Usung heroes are the most exciting and often the most challenging of the breeds—bizarre, hard-to-find, unearthed by the most erudite scholars in the various BP departments.

It's painful to recount the number of videos we endured in an effort to seek out the few, the proud, the unsung.

Dinner is served.

Allegro Non Troppo

The Italian Fantasia.

Ravel. Fucking . . . Ravel. There's only one explanation for the brilliance of his music. He was a traveler from the far and distant future who was present on the fields of Armageddon when Gabriel blew his golden horn to an unbearably patient melody that sung the death knell of the race of beings that the Creator made in Its own image and taped the whole damn thing like a concert bootleg and brought it back a thousand years in time to give those who lived in the decaying civilization that was Olde Europe something beautiful to listen to as it died. He called it *Bolero,* and we don't mean John Derek's embarrassing testimonial to wife Bo's naked body. We mean Ravel! In *Allegro Non Troppo,* the filmmakers put animation that's just as patient and well-crafted as the music in perfect rhythm with the driving beat of the song. When it's over, all you'll be left with is a plate of Frito-Lays where your head used to be. Ravel.

Oh yeah . . . there's a bunch of other animated shorts put to classical music in the movie, and some goofy live-action stuff in between, which acts as a video sorbet. Come down from the intensity of each passing short and regather your strength to avoid the fatigue that inevitably ruins any viewing of *Fantasia.*

All that stuff is pretty good, but it's not Ravel.

1976 (75 min.). Voice of Maurizio Nichetti. Dir.: Bruno Bozzetto.

     VL

The Bear

An orphaned bear cub tries to cope with life in the wild without his mother.

For ninety-five minutes, this Disneyesque animal adventure walks hand-in-hand with wildlife footage from even the best of your late-night Discovery Channel binges. It conjures up the glory days when they were still making those "let's get back to the woods" flicks like *The Life and Times of Grizzly Adams* and *The Adventures of the Wilderness Family*. Mother Nature never lets you down. The cub goes through all the pains of growing up while you kick back and enjoy the process of forgetting them.

However, it isn't just the spectacular footage that makes *The Bear* a sage choice. Director Jean-Jacques Annaud somehow managed to slip one of the greatest drug sequences in screen history into a children's flick. The lucky little cub stumbles upon a thriving patch of mushrooms, and darned if they don't do funny things to his head! Annaud makes the hallucinations vivid enough to trigger that latent acid hiding in your fatty tissue. We owe thanks to lenient censors for a change.

1989 (93 min.). Bart, Douce, Jack Wallace, Tcheky Karyo, Andre Lacombe. Dir.: Jean-Jacques Annaud.

 VS

Big Trouble in Little China

Something to do with Chinese mythology, martial arts, girls with green eyes, and a truck.

Here's how things work in the *Big Trouble* universe. All white people are loud, obnoxious fools, represented by wisecracking trucker and tough-guy extraordinaire Kurt Russell. And everyone of even remotely Asian descent is a bonafide expert in all forms of the martial arts. *Everyone*. We'll let those politically correct members of the audience decide whether this kind of stereotyping is funny or racist (or both). In the Baked Potatoes universe, we are above such petty moral judgments, concerning ourselves only with the vital issues. Such as whether or not the movie enhances or detracts from our high, or how the mounds of pot we were forced to buy during the research of this book can be written off on our taxes.

As for the movie in question? The plot stops making sense about the same time the dialogue does, and you get the sense that they were making things up as they went along, but somehow John Carpenter's martial arts/sci-fi/fantasy/action/adventure flick comes out on top. It's like watching a good jazz ensemble improvise. Sometimes they hit, sometimes they miss, but you have to admire the effort. And if you're patient, they'll usually reward you with a few tender morsels of ecstasy. *Big Trouble in Little China* has more than enough to go around.

1986 (99 min.). Kurt Russell, Kim Cattrall, Dennis Dun, James Hong, Victor Wong. Dir.: John Carpenter.

The Blizzard of AAHHHs: A True Story 🍁 🍁 🍁

Powder-filled, sun-blazed, snow-covered, ripping-bright-blue ski mayhem.

It's 7:00 A.M. and a helicopter in British Columbia just dropped you on the top of a huge, deserted glacier with twenty-two inches of fresh powder. You put on your skis, slide to the ledge of the cliff, and look down. Your vision's blocked by the clouds . . . under you. You're one of the three best skiers in the world and the other two guys are shaking their heads no way. You have a fourteen-inch, bleach-blond mohawk and you're not scared of shit. You're insane. People are around you with cameras, waiting to see if you'll jump off the cliff, catch forty feet of air, and potentially survive. You creep up to the ledge and slowly look around with a smile, greeting each nervous face as you turn. You shake your head, laugh out loud at the tiny and weak, and jump. And you're baked out of your fucking mind.

Welcome to The Blizzard. *The Blizzard of AAHHHs*. And the title's no joke. Glen Plake, Mike Hattrup, and cliff jumper Scott Schmidt in some of the best extreme/steep-skiing sequences ever committed to film. Producer, director, writer, editor, BP visionary Greg Stump (Warren Miller on acid) delivers yet another storm of the freshly packed blotter. Alpha Blondy and other well-chosen musical trails only enhance and respark the high-energy back bowls of the day.

If only it really was you? With four good speakers, proper supplies, and the right frame of mind . . . it is.

   Also available from Greg Stump Productions: the slightly more hardcore *License to Thrill* (complete with preprogrammed bong re-up intermissions), *Groove Requiem, Dr. Strangeglove, The Maltese Flamingo, Pulp Traction* (mountain biking), *The Good, the Rad, and the Gnarly, Time Waits for Snowman,* and the latest ski-bound offering, *P-Tex, Lies, and Duct Tape.* All highest, worth-every-penny, must-see *quality.* Greg Stump order line: 1-800-356-4558.

1988 (75 min.). Glen Plake, Mike Hattrup, Scott Schmidt. Dir.: Greg Stump.

Brainstorm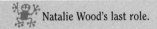

Baked Potato virtual-reality-fest veiled in techno-thriller sheep's clothing.

There's something about being high and Christopher Walken that seem to go hand in hand. Hard to put a finger on it, but you can just tell. Some actors welcome the Baked Potato. Others push him or her away. That's what that Stanislavsky guy was all into. All about different methods. The carrot, the soda can, the five-hosed Indian hookah with party bowl. Accept the pot smoker and you accept yourself.

That's what *Brainstorm* is all about, too. Scientists Walken and Fletcher invent a means to record experience and play it back as experience. That's right. In the *Brainstorm*ian world you could record the pleasure of reading *Baked Potatoes* and send it to your infant nephew just in time for his third birthday.

Defense Department arrives, begins packaging said device for military use, and locks Walken out. So they think. *Brainstorm* caps an already impressive scane with an especially nice end sequence. Louise Fletcher dies with the machine on, recording her ascent toward the afterlife. Walken finds the reel and presses *play*.

 Natalie Wood's last role.

1983 (106 min.). Natalie Wood, Christopher Walken, Cliff Robertson, Louise Fletcher. Dir.: Douglas Trumbull.

VS

A Brief History of Time

Baked guy in wheelchair figures out universe.

Most of us can relate to those moments when we've figured out the entire universe and swear the next morning we'll write it all down. Finally, after all this time and energy, after all these idiot philosophers, you've figured out the universe, here on this giant empty field, with just a twig in your hand and Jerry in the background. Incredible.

Stephen Hawking had that feeling for more than six to twelve hours. This guy had the balls to publish a book called *A Brief History of Time.* Think about that. "I went to the Blimpie interview, Mom, now don't bother me, I'm working on a brief history of time in here. Yeah, Dinospaghettios are great."

Well, the documentary is pretty much mind-bending. Stephen Hawking has a touch of amyotrophic lateral sclerosis that forces him into odd shapes and a wheelchair and to talk out of a computer, but once you get used to it, you'll stop convulsing. Then tune into the history of the universe, complete with getting sucked in and crushed by black holes, randomness, entropy, and predictions for the rise of a vegetable-oriented people with blue turbans.

1992 (84 min.). Stephen Hawking. Mus.: Philip Glass. Dir.: Errol Morris.

The Brother from Another Planet 🌿 🌿 🌿 🌿

Dennis Rodman.

Supposedly they're gonna have five hundred channels soon. Great. Four hundred QVCs and the Nashville Network. They're also gonna have on-command, interactive movie selection, where you can just rent off the TV. The BP Foreign Lobbyists are campaigning for a "Baked" section on the server, but so far it's an uphill battle. We're trying to tack it onto the DARE legislation, but the Republicans keep calling it "pork." If that's not the pot calling the kettle black.

The point being, *The Brother from Another Planet*. An alien slave escapes captors and ends up in Harlem pursued by two bounty hunters from his home world. A fascinating and independent, off-the-beaten-track, shoestring budget adventure that just reeks of Baked Potato pride. Urban, dirty, nonfluff.

1984 (104 min.). Joe Morton, Dee Dee Bridgewater, Ren Woods. Dir.: John Sayles.

  ♪ 🎟 VL

Cafe Flesh 🌿 🌿 🌿 🌿

A place to go when caffeine-enriched soft drinks just won't do.

Like the skinny redheaded stepchild some of us lock in our basements, today's chain video stores have turned their backs on the venerable art form that first jump-started the industry. Exiled it to the dusty corner behind the green curtain; embarrassed to recognize its contribution to a more . . . liberal world. But ever so slowly, things are changing. The realm of adult films is no longer solely inhabited by fat, balding, middle-aged perverts with sweaty, eager palms. Men and—yes—women of all ages have opened their minds to the simple pleasure of watching someone else do it better then they can. Amongst the collection of low-budget home-video and grainy-genitalia exhibits, this art-house favorite rises to the top as the *Citizen Kane* of smut. Watch other people watching people get laid, and think about what it all means. Ruminate. Philosophize. Enjoy the one true porn flick geared specifically for both the horny and the high. And keep your hands where everyone can see 'em.

Should only be rented in groups of three or more, so the kid behind the counter doesn't get any wrong ideas.

1982 (80 min.). Dir.: Rinse Dream.

     F

GUEST REVIEW

Reviewer:
Wavy Gravy
Occupation:
Baked Potato icon/activist/musician/guru/ice cream flavor.

Cisco Pike 🌿 🌿 🌿 🌿

Washed-up rock star blackmailed by corrupt narcotics agent.

You know, *High Times* had me on the cover as the Prince of Pot, and I run summer camps—the Rainbow Camps—so, you know, all these parents started getting freaked-out, like their kids were gonna turn into hippies and freaks, all this stuff that is probably a lot better than a lot of other things you could turn into, so I wasn't able to smoke pot anymore in public and all this stuff so I really shouldn't be doing this guest review at all, you know, all this bullshit starts catching up with you. But then again, who gives a shit?

This is a really excellent movie because not only is it great to see high, but it covers the subject of getting high and covers it intelligently. In addition, it also features yours truly, Wavy Gravy, in action as the naive hippie commune leader . . . which immediately establishes the film as a cult classic. The entire personnel of the Hog Farm were extras in the film, but for unspecified reasons this ended up on the editing-room floor.

Not only does *Cisco Pike* feature some of Kris's best tunes, but it establishes him firmly and finally as the Aquarian Humphrey Bogart. Enter the first true-to-life consumption of cannabis and the consummation of hip sex, banishing the ludicrous portrayals of drugs and sex in film perpetrated previous to this point.

> He's a problem when he's high . . .
> A walking contradiction
> Partly fact, partly fiction . . .

A nice dose of Karen Black whose romance with Kris is beautiful. Don't miss the scene where Karen's in the lotus position, doing some yoga postures, going "ohmmm," and Kris comes around and grabs her breasts and goes "ohmmmm." Definitely a date movie, done in what I would call good-bad taste.

Mexican weed for preparation—it's that time frame and pays homage to everyone who remembers Mexican keys wrapped in wax paper. However, this is not a bad movie, so you don't *have* to get zonked out of your mind to enjoy it. Unless you should so choose.

Great moments with Kris on the phone, trying to move these keys around L.A.

I don't know if you get it on video, but it's a fucking excellent movie. I give it three and a half potatoes. No, screw that, four potatoes.

Wavy says check it out.

1972 (94 min.). Kris Kristofferson, Karen Black, Gene Hackman, Harry Dean Stanton. Dir.: B. W. L. Norton.

 H

Clambake 🌿 🌿 🌿

The King swings, swivels, and serenades the babes at the beach.

To be quite honest, we could just as well have included any Elvis vehicle with equal conviction. They're all the same generally; the only true differentiating factor is the degree of Elvis's mental and physical decay. There was a strong movement for the addition of *Viva Las Vegas,* but most of us found Ann-Margret's frenzied style of dance profoundly disturbing. Thus, we recommend this film, one of the final pieces of excess from a truly excessive career. The Big E has finally crossed the line in this mind-numbing musical extravaganza. *Extravaganza* is a word that can only be used with a straight face if Elvis is involved. It conjures up all the right images. Throbbing neon lights. Poorly made-up women with blue beehives on their heads, Southern accents on their tongues, and velvet paintings clutched in their horny little hands. A hunka, hunka burnin' love in an ever-expanding selection of white polyester. *Clambake* must be treasured simply for the thought of who was in the audience during its disappointing theatrical run, and, more important, for giving us an Elvis immersed in the virgin throes of depression and painkiller addiction.

It's "America, the Beautiful." It's professional wrestling, the sad careers of ex-MTV VJs, and the Jungle Room all rolled into one. It's the King. Bake your clam, add just the right helping of Velveeta (not enough to upset your tummy), and go home satisfied.

1967 (97 min.). Elvis Presley, Shelley Fabares, Bill Bixby. Dir.: Arthur Nadel.

  F

Crimes and Misdemeanors

Concurrent and eventually intersecting stories of a schleppy filmmaker and his struggles and a highly regarded ophthalmologist whose mistress threatens to reveal him.

Like gefilte fish, Woody Allen can be a risky call. You either love it or you can't believe people actually eat that jelly-coated pummus. Or you don't even know what it is, in which case it's worth asking your local grocer. Supermarkets are such bizarre places. All these people milling about in public solitude. Everyone's got their baskets and their little preferences in their baskets. You can tell a lot about a person by his or her grocery basket. If it's a different color or size or has more wheels than all the other baskets, the person probably brought it from home. A little neurotic. If he or she has an entire basket of baking potatoes, this is good: poor and stoned. If he or she has more than one tin of Spam, this is not good: may have a satellite dish but probably knits toilet-paper holders out of human skin.

Every film you see, someone's falling in love in the supermarket. This is called "suspension of disbelief." The only people you ever run into in the supermarket are people you absolutely do not want to see.

Now, *Crimes and Misdemeanors* may seem like an odd choice. The humor's there, but more pronounced is the utterly brilliant and subtle account of the characters and their general struggle with morality and self. One of Allen's most serious films, but so good it just can't be overlooked. May sound dry but all the better for rolling.

1989 (104 min.). Martin Landau, Woody Allen, Alan Alda, Mia Farrow, Anjelica Huston, Sam Waterston, Daryl Hannah, Nora Ephron. Dir.: Woody Allen.

          VS

Delicatessen

A landlord in ye olde postapocalyptic nightmare world runs out of cold cuts and is forced to seek a new source of meat to feed his hungry tenants...themselves.

A plateful of grilled cheese sandwiches, pipin' hot. Derek and the Dominos, *The Jams, #4.* Making sure the remote has fresh batteries. Disconnecting the phone. Keeping the bong at the center of the table. A long, hot shower. Hiding the book depicting the work of H. R. Giger. A large bottle of European spring water. Buying a bag that ain't running out any time soon. Finding a fueled lighter. Locking down a good seat. Reading *Giving Tree.*

Wise decisions on any pot-smoking eve. And if chopping up those annoying neighbors and tossing them on a baguette with some Muenster and a thin slice of onion is your sort of thing, and we're pretty sure it is, then *Delicatessen* is the film for you. Easily the funniest film about cannibalism ever made.

1991 (95 min.). Marie-Laure Dougnac, Dominique Pinon, Karin Viard, Jean Claude Dreyfus. Dir.: Jean-Pierre Jeunet, Marc Caro.

Dellamorte Dellamore

It starts with a cemetery caretaker fighting to keep the dead from coming back to life. Where it goes from there, your guess is as good as ours.

Wanna play a trick on that pot leech that everybody knows? That fixture at every bake session who has never bought a bag, packed a bowl, rolled a joint, or pistol-whipped a hippie who is late on his payments, yet always materializes in that third or fourth spot in the smoking order. Sound familiar? If so, then invite the leech over with a bunch of friends, spike the pot with a little touch of the Northern Lights, and fire up *Dellamorte Dellamore*.

Why? Because the story behind this ultra-hard-to-find Italian epic is told in such a bizarre, stream-of-consciousness manner that you can't possibly understand what's happening or what will happen next. The whole way through you keep waiting for the film to start and then you realize, this *is* the film. Kind of like life. Accept it early and don't try too hard, there's enough hilarious, over-the-top gore and insanely beautiful photography to more than carry the day. But struggle to comprehend the madness? Ah-hah . . .

The inevitable moment will arrive when the leech is forced to publicly state, "Is anyone else as lost as I am?" Yank the rug out. All you have to say is, "No, I'm following it pretty well." If necessary, someone else can offer, "What's wrong? Did you smoke too much?" Everybody else should laugh in inappropriate places, and nod knowingly as if it's all starting to make sense. Then sit back and view the fireworks, as the leech futiley attempts to gather up all the loose plot strings, without the knowledge that the filmmakers themselves never bothered to tie them. A dirty trick? Absolutely. But as they say, you get what you pay for.

Based on the novel by Tiziano Sclavi. Published by Camunia. Edited versions released in some countries as *The Cemetery Man*.

1994 (100 min.). Rupert Everett, Francois Hadji Lazaro, Anna Falchi. Dir.: Michele Soavi.

Destroy All Monsters!

The king of the monsters teams up with his ex-enemies to face a common threat.

Remember the 4:30 Movie? For fifty-one weeks each year, we were treated to a worthless collection of pseudoclassics grouped loosely by genre, over-the-hill leading man, or costumed ape flick. But there was that one special week. If you weren't careful, it slipped by unnoticed. The only way to be sure was to watch the end of every Friday edition, to check what next week held in store. And when it came around? Five days of nirvana. Do we have to say its name? Do we have to speak its name? MONSTER WEEK!!!!!!!!!!!!!!!!

Godzilla, Rodan, Mothra . . . Gammera the flying turtle if we ate our veggies and said our prayers at night. And on Friday afternoon, the coup de grâce. *D.A.M.* All the big players, plus minor leaguers Spiga, Angillus, and chip-off-the-old-block Minya (no, his name wasn't Godzookie), united under the firm, steady leadership of moviedom's greatest anti-hero. Together for one final battle against that crumb Monster Zero, Ghydera to his pals in the freaky spacesuits. Relive it. Summer break, Christmas, and all eight days of Hanukkah wrapped into one.

P.S. Suspension of disbelief is key ingredient. Those guys in rubber suits looked a lot cooler in third grade.

1968 (88 min.). Akira Kubo, Jun Tazaki, Yoshio Tsuchiya. Dir.: Ishiro Honda.

Diva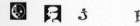

It's like the What's Happening!! where Rerun gets caught bootlegging the Doobies, but European.

We know what you're thinking. "A French movie? With subtitles? Clearly you idiots have no idea what you're talking about!" It's understandable. The fear of foreign films has its roots in the religious right and the mass media's propaganda assault on the average pot smoker. They've instilled an inferiority complex that tells us we've killed too many of the brain cells we need to follow films in which we can't understand what the actors are saying without reading the teeny-tiny little words at the bottom of the screen. As Lou Reed so aptly put it, "Don't believe half of what you see, and none of what you hear."

Unless what you see and hear comes from (insert deep voice-over of announcer from "unclaimed freight" commercials) BAKED POTATOES! This romantic thriller, about the battle for control of a bootlegged opera tape, is the perfect film for those inevitable nights when you're starting to worry that getting high, binging on pizza-flavored Cheese-filled Combos, watching movies, and sleeping while in a sitting position isn't as cool as it used to be. *Diva* is so hip, Eurotrashy, and stylish that it can only be experienced to full effect in a black turtleneck with slicked-back hair. Watch it, and you'll be hip and Eurotrashy, too. As for stylish? You smoke pot, friend . . . you already have style.

1982 (123 min.). Wilhelmenia Wiggins Fernandez, Frederic Andrei, Richard Bohringer, Thuy An Luu, Jacques Fabbri. Dir.: Jean-Jacques Beineix.

Doctor Detroit II: The Wrath of Mom

The return of that wacky pimp and his collection of beautiful pros.

The most eagerly awaited sequel since *The Empire Strikes Back*. Alright, so the film hasn't come out yet, and isn't likely to. But all of us Detroitophiles refuse to believe that we will never again hear the words "Never with the Doctor . . . Never!" Shall we just fantasize for a moment about what high jinks might be included in this fun-filled follow up? Perhaps we learn how and why Dan Aykroyd was a lean, mean, comic machine in the late seventies and now plays a various assortment of fat nerds in bad comedies (we're quite sure the doctors at The Clinic said, "Stop doing so much coke, Mr. Aykroyd," and not, "Stop being funny . . ."). Or maybe we'll find out how exactly he managed to swing Donna Dixon. And if we're truly lucky, we'll even get to sing along as Dapper Dan does one of his classic, hip-white-boy musical numbers. *The Wrath of Mom* will be the comeback vehicle that all *SNL* fans knew *Loose Cannons* could've been, if only it had been . . . watchable.

1997 (101 min.). Dan Aykroyd, Donna Dixon, Howard Hesseman, Fran Drescher, Sir Laurence Olivier. Dir.: Sir Laurence Olivier.

      H

Dreamscape

Baked Potato saves world.

There's always some ass-head around to explain to you how he knows for a fact that if you're falling in a dream and you hit the ground and die, you die in real life. Generally, this is the same individual who insists Arnold has eight Ph.D.'s, *Hangar 18* was true, and he personally knows the guy from the Batman-in-the-closet story. Arnold has eight Ph.D.'s and he's into fitness. Big fucking deal. Bruce Jenner was into fitness, and have you seen him lately? Not pretty.

Dennis Quaid couldn't care less. He stars in the underrated unicorn of dreamworld battalia. Doctor von Sydow teaches wunderkind Quaid to enter sleep and repair patient's nightmares, but evil-student-turned-Ginsu makes guest appearance and slices/dices victim's watermelon subconscious.

It's hard to know who to root for. Especially when you realize who the villain is. Ginsu Man was in *48 HRS.* and, most notably, was the Getty Lee-esque, clinking gang-leader extraordinaire from *The Warriors*.

Good vs. evil. Always a tough choice.

1984 (99 min.). Dennis Quaid, Max von Sydow, Christopher Plummer, Eddie Albert, David Patrick Kelly. Dir.: Joseph Ruben.

 VS

The Element of Crime

A man searches for a killer of young girls in yet another postapocalyptic nightmare world.

The Element of Crime is a brilliant depiction of a dystopian future, with a climax that deserves major kudos for sheer suspense and horror. It's a world where blacks and whites and colors have faded with civilization, and all that is left is the brown of destruction. The film explores the mind of a twisted murderer who could only emerge from such a place. It's a movie that will stick in your craw long after it's over. It's very hard to let go after such an intense experience, to separate yourself. The carryover is, well . . . it's these thoughts . . . they just don't disappear on their own, you know. You can try and try and try, but they're not gonna . . . did you ever walk through a maternity ward and see all the beaming mommies with their brand-new baby boys and girls? Did you ever think about grabbing a cute little child, and before the mother could do a god-damn thing take that sweet bundle of joy by its soft, rubbery feet and smash it down on the hard floor with everything you got? Would it explode like a pumpkin dropped off the Empire State Building or just crack in the manner of a fresh coconut? What would it sound like? And wouldn't that look of abject horror, that "Oh my God, WHAT HAVE YOU DONE TO MY BABY!" expression on the stunned parents' faces be something to treasure for as long as you lived? Or until the day you did it again? It would make life on the run worth living, don't you think? Or better yet, take the kid, bury it up to its neck in the soft earth some forty-five yards away from the goalposts, and imagine you're Scott Norwood, only this time the kick is good! Bills win the Super Bowl, 22–20! Admit it! You've thought about it, right? Don't lie to yourself! It's you! Admit it!

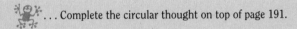 . . . Complete the circular thought on top of page 191.

1985 (104 min.). Michael Elphick, Esmond Knight, Me Me Lei. Dir.: Lars Von Trier.

Fearless 🌿 🌿 🌿 🌿

Story of plane-crash survivor and his efforts to deal with the unusual psychological trauma. And strawberries.

Getting on a plane is a little like tripping. Once you take off, there's no sense worrying; it's out of your hands. The possibility for disaster does exist and once you realize this it becomes all the more likely. And once you realize that, it becomes even more likely. And once you realize *that,* please consult Appendix II.

A largely overlooked jewel, Peter Weir's *(The Last Wave)* super kind is a burner in pig's clothing. Big-budget studio release with an independent heart. *Fearless* takes the standard and blows the expected to pieces. Even

Rosie Perez, normally unbearable, grasps at decent . . . but fails. The end of *Fearless,* a full fifteen-minute, no-dialogue plane-crash collage, is astounding. Easily the best ever filmed.

Don't watch this if (a) it's the in-flight feature, or (b) you just came back from Appendix II. Read the USAir magazine instead. They have this new gadget that steams your cummerbund and assassinates pop vocalists at the same time.

1993 (122 min.). Jeff Bridges, Isabella Rossellini, Rosie Perez. Dir.: Peter Weir.

     VS

Fishtrucks 🍁 🍁 🍁 🍁

A small fish wholesaler finds himself in possession of some very special seafood.

Perhaps the greatest feature film never made. The bidding war that surrounded this remarkable script is legendary. It was so bloody, in fact, that the rights to produce it are tied up in civil courts until midway through the next century. We all know what happens when the Griffin Millses of the world option a brilliant project, promise big things, then bury it in memoranda and "This is a big week for *Fishtrucks"*–like statements. But if you're lucky, if you're really in the know, you can get your hands on a bootleg copy of the short film that inspired the entire Hollywood fiasco. The simple, tragicomic story of Salvatore and the "altered" fish that changed his life also comes with a shock ending for which absolutely nothing can prepare you. What happens? We're not telling. *Fishtrucks* dominated the small festival circuit, inspiring a cult so loyal and thorough that each videotape has been signed, numbered, and can only be watched legally in the presence of both filmmakers and their counsel. It'll cost you dearly, but if you want the best, you've gotta pay for it. Fishtruckies and black marketeers know what we mean. Our VCR scoffs at the law at least two nights a week. And at you.

For information contact Jed Alpert on the BP Legal Defense Team.

1991 (27 min.). Bob Kertes, Franklin Cipot, Edward Leppert, John Powell. Dir.: Robert Knoll, H. P. Owl.

Gates of Heaven

Ostensibly, a documentary about pet cemeteries and the personalities and pets who inhabit them.

In reality, an album of some of the most subtle and brilliant portraits of pure, uncensored human animals ever filmed. No writer could hope to pen the dialogue or develop the characters contained within *Gates of Heaven*. And even if one succeeded, no actor in history could even come close to pulling off the performance.

The setting—pet cemeteries—only highlights the strange and profound terrain in which all of these characters, from the cemetery owners to the rendering service employees, battle to construct intricate and complex systems of beliefs by which their lives can somehow be rationalized. And it's not because they work at the cemetery.

Intercut the intensity with the tragicomedy of tear-ridden, funeral-attending pet owners and you still can't imagine where the *Gates of Heaven* lead.

Masterpiece.

Beware the woman in the doorway . . .
Not to be confused with Michael Cimino's *Heaven's Gate*.
Other quality Errol Morris: *Vernon, Florida, The Thin Blue Line, A Brief History of Time.*

1978 (85 min.). Dir.: Errol Morris.

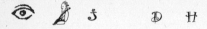

The Grave (aka The Secret)

Rednecks hunt Civil War graveyard booty.

Still unreleased at the time of frying, *The Grave* represents a major breakthrough in Baked Potato history. Not only do the characters roast incessantly (rumor of producorial drug fetish filtered into script). Not only do we witness the long-awaited Anthony Michael Hall comeback, as he's rescued, forever more, maybe, from projects the likes of *A Gnome Named Gnorm.* Not only are we privy to the magical choreography and superior architect's eye of precocious, first-time wunderkind director Jonas Pate. But *Baked Potatoes,* the book you are now reading, is actually featured in this film.

Sure, there's something to be said for the surreality of a *Blade Runner. Star Wars* had its moments. *Animal House* had some cheap laughs. And they got their five-leaf ratings. However, there is one quality that transcends petty artistic genius. And that's product placement using *Baked Potatoes.*

Hence, the only six-leaf review.

Buried treasure, buried people, swamps, prisons, black comedy, high quality. And a guy named Cletus.

Watch for never-released *BP* front cover in poker scene.

This review dedicated to the family of *The Grave* set PA struck by lightning during shooting.

A Peter Glatzer production.

1996 (99 min.). Craig Sheffer, Gabrielle Anwar, Josh Charles, Anthony Michael Hall, Keith David, Eric Roberts, Donal Logue, Max Perlich. Dir.: Jonas Pate.

H

Hearts of Darkness: A Filmmaker's Apocalypse

The making of Apocalypse Now.

Remember Ismelda Marcos had that whole closet full of like five hundred pairs of shoes and the entire country was eating beef jerky and starving? That's what happens when a Baked Potato goes awry. One minute your roasting at a Dead show, the next day you wake up the tan, squat wife of a Filipino dictator.

How does it feel to be stuck in the Philippines and confused? *Hearts of Darkness* follows Francis Coppola and documents the emotional, fascinating production of *Apocalypse Now*. Complete with stolen audio and video footage shot by his wife Eleanor, ramblings by the strung-out, passionate director, and interviews with the cast and crew (minus Brando, who declined), *Apocalypse* aficionados and other curious kids will dig this island delight.

Brando declines? Who do you think you are, pal? You were in *The Freshman* with a Kamoto dragon. Kneel before Potato Zod.

> Classic, molto-bizarro scene of drunken and bleeding Martin Sheen falling apart on camera.

1991 (96 min.). Sam Bottoms, Eleanor Coppola, Francis Ford Coppola, Robert Duvall, Laurence Fishburne, Frederic Forrest, Albert Hall, Den-

*nis Hopper, George Lucas, John Milius, Martin Sheen. Dir.: Fax Bahr,
George Hickenlooper.*

   D   VL

House of Games

**Female psychiatrist sucked into realm of sophisticated con
masters.**

David Mamet's first film is something dangerously close to brilliant.
Dialogue, plot, cinematography—unequivocally a well-Baked Potato.
And they don't come easy. It's a one-timer, though, so you've only got
one time to make it count. Now, listen carefully. Set aside two hours and
mark it on your schedule. On the appointed day arrive at the video store
and request it by name. Don't read the box. Don't ask what it's about.

Turn off the ringer. Unplug the machine. Close the blinds. Talkers,
pausers, people who always have to piss need not attend. *House of Games*
demands and deserves your undivided attention. Offer the proper respect
and you shall be rewarded.

Professionals only.

*1987 (102 min.). Joe Mantegna, Lindsay Crouse, Lilia Skala, J. T. Walsh.
Dir.: David Mamet.*

      j   VL   VS

Incident at Oglala: The Leonard Peltier Story

The real conspiracy.

Acid users in jail longer than rapists? Bush pardons Caspar Cheeseburger the day before he leaves office? Reagan didn't know about Iran-Contra? Give us a break, a senile actor could have remembered that.

Narrated by Robert Redford, Michael Apted's documentary traces the Leonard Peltier story, one of the more vivid travesties of justice in recent times. Peltier, a Native American activist framed by the FBI for the alleged murder of Bureau boys, is still serving two life sentences for the events of the South Dakota shoot-out. Amnesty International lists him as a political prisoner.

Even Nancy herself would be shocked by the obscene, abominable lies of the astrologically illiterate FBI. Like a long-haired grip on a film set once said: "Karma comes back around and doles out the death knell." It's true, but this incident sends you applying for assistant doler. Jarring and unreal.

Derived largely from Peter Matthiessen's *In the Spirit of Crazy Horse*. Check it out.

1992 (89 min.). Dir.: Michael Apted.

J&B on the Rox

Cable-access television show/video series featuring adventures/insidious machinations of Indiana-based stoners.

J&B on the Rox is damn entertaining. Basically, it's J, Your Bartender, B, Your Editor, and people you know, calling bullshit on police moronhood, scoffing at the absurdity of society in general, doing pointless but funny shit, taping it, editing it, putting music in it, and somehow airing it as a weekly public-access television show in Bloomington, Indiana. Smashing pumpkins, getting baked in the woods, running naked and getting arrested, interviewing bloated and embarrassingly sad police and local officials. *Absolutely, positively* worth the cost of admission. Here's some info direct from the heartland:

Who is Rox?

"We might be described as a ragtag association of media artists, drug dealers, technogeeks, and just plain folx. There is no fixed roster or membership—this is not a club. We don't hold official positions or titles—there is nothing "official" about Rox. But we persist and even succeed for some reason. Go figure."

ROX 59: "J&B Get Baked."

In which we came out of the closet and announced our rampant stonerdom to the world. *(30 min.)*

ROX 64: "The Overt Promotion of Anarchy."

Part of the aftermath of "J&B Get Baked." The Governor's Commission for a Drug-Free Indiana accused us of the "overt promotion of anarchy" and took steps to shut us down. Thankfully the First Amendment still means something, at least for the time being, and this episode is a testament to that. *(30 min.)*

"Alan and Glenda's Wedding."

Oops. I dubbed this by accident—let the tape run too long. Fast-forward unless you're stoned enough to trip out on someone else's wedding video. *(20 min.)*

One tape of three episodes costs $19.95 plus shipping. Over eighty-five episodes to date. Indiana residents add 5 percent sales tax to any tapes ordered. Call The LodesTone Catalog, 1-800-411-MIND, to place a credit card order, or send check or money order to Smiling Dog Video, P.O. Box 3241, Bloomington, IN 47402. WWW: http://www.rox.com/quarry/. E-mail: b@rox.com.

Quality.

ʮ

The Kids Are Alright

Rock-bio/documentary of musical group The Who.

BPAC Chairman Ted Pryde was advocating this little gem since day one. Unfortunately, in their excessively baked states of mind, certain members of BP Central resisted the calling. Whispers began as a result of the rift, BP Intelligence reporting in closed session that Chairman Pryde had lost his wits and with them his trademark sixth sense of movie acumen. Even those loyal to Pryde threatened suicide if they were forced to hear "Happy Jack" yet again.

On the final night of BP screening, the fiery chairman showed up tape-in-hand and exercised his God-given right. Glances shot about the room, but out of respect the tape was allowed to roll.

The chairman proved as masterful as ever, reminding all in the room of his awesome qualifications.

The kids were alright. More than alright. A lot more than alright. Keith Moon? The guy is out of his mind. You might not think about it, but watching a drummer tear beyond comprehension when you're baked is a righteous pleasure.

Combine Moon with Pete Townshend, *on fire,* Daltrey not afraid to work the rock-god angle, and darkhorse genius John Entwistle—you're in store for a major unsung hero. Contrary to the packaged sound, which radio hits like "Can't Explain" and "My Generation" perpetrated, these guys jammed beyond belief and destroyed their equipment with unparalleled style. Even better than that, they destroyed every reporter who tried to communicate with them. One interview that weaves through the entire film is, by far, the most absurd display of maniacal-and-incoherent-band-members trying to be reasoned with by minion-of-ordinary-society that you have ever seen. Keith Moon drops his pants and rips Pete Townshend's shirtsleeve off while the interviewer flounders like a dead hippo. Unreal.

Also included: insight into the band's inner dynamics and their evolution over time; concert footage that kicks; and the most mind-boggling light show/guitar jam "Won't Get Fooled Again" mind-blow known to mankind. This climax is so high, musically and emotionally, as Townshend comes full circle from thrash teenager to artiste espousing the silliness of smashing his guitar to smashing it anyway in the end.

Keith Moon sums it all up after taunting another interviewer with fellow drunk Ringo Starr for a half hour. The reporter comes back in the room, finds Moon alone, and says to him something to the effect of "Why don't you tell us the truth now." Moon looks at him and responds, "I can't do that. I can't tell you the truth . . . the way you want to hear it. You can't afford me."

If you didn't already know, you'll have a whole new opinion of The Who.

Must-see.

1979 (108 min.). Dir.: Jeff Stein.

Koyaanisqatsi

Hypnotic and truly unique look at modern life through music, landscapes, and cityscapes.

Translated from the Hopi Indian, "life out of balance," Francis Ford Coppola's production of *Koyaanisqatsi* is a blatant masterpiece, a radical, incomparable vision of reality and the seething chaos and energy that underlie existence.

From the day of its release, filmgoers have cited the watching of *Koyaanisqatsi* as a religious experience and instigator of deep-seeded epiphany. The slow, mesmerizing visuals tap into that haze in the center of your soul, morphing and twisting to your own self-imposed patterns.

Optimum conditions are crucial: big-size screen, dark quiet room, and extensive help from the green gremlin. Not watching this high is a tragic error, and you absolutely must step over the line. Take that extra toke you usually don't and let go.

No dialogue. No actors. No script. Just a Philip Glass score and the swarming cinematography of natural forces.

What's inside?
In the words of Yoda, "Only what you take with you."

1983 (87 min.). Mus.: Philip Glass. Dir.: Godfrey Reggio.

Labyrinth

Kids take acid while mom's away, end up in maze with David Bowie and The Muppets.

Labyrinth has a lot of David Bowie, and it's hard to know exactly how to respond to that. Kind of like being promoted to VP but reassigned to the Detroit office.

There's a few ways to cope: (a) suicide—clean, simple, lots of pity, and insurance; (b) total midlife-crisis move to Colorado, become pothead; (c) take out on little brother and wish Goblin King, Bowie, to come grab tyke because baby-sitting chunks.

Jennifer Connelly chose *c* and look what happened. No Detroit. She ended up in giant 3-D labyrinth, searching for little Toby before his switch to permanent goblinhood. Screw podiatry, this is a real job! Thank Kermit for Jim Henson, whose furry, kooky creatures populate the maze and help us all enjoy the day most handsomely.

Executive-produced by George Lucas, written by Monty Python's Terry Jones, sixty-four colors and the sharpener.

1986 (101 min.). David Bowie, Jennifer Connelly, Toby Froud. Dir.: Jim Henson.

The Last Wave 🍁 🍁 🍁

Richard Chamberlain and his visions of the apocalypse in Australia.

There are two kinds of weird. Intentionally weird, like an Obsession ad. Or genuinely fucking bizarre. Out there. Downright strange. Like Jesse Helms. True weirdness is something to be relished. Peter Weir's feature-film debut definitely inhabits this rarefied air. It's like taking a weekend vacation to the Bizarro World with Mr. Mxyzypltyk as your tour guide. The less you know about the story, the better. It's very slow at some points, but have the courage to stick it out for the ultimate pay-off. As BP classics *Total Recall, Predator,* and almost all entries by John Carpenter unfortunately illustrate, finding the right way to put a movie to bed is not an easy trick. *The Last Wave* is one of the few and the proud. It delivers a coup de grâce of the highest order, and that's lucky, because it might be the only part that you won't need explained to you at a later date. And always remember to say Kytlpyzyxm before you stop the tape.

1977 (106 min.). Richard Chamberlain, Olivia Hamnett. Dir.: Peter Weir.

Laws of Gravity 🍁 🍁 🍁

Three turbulent days in the lives of young, working-class Brooklyn hoods and their girlfriends.

The performances in this movie are incredible; almost as baffling as why a small ball falls from a rooftop at the same rate as a large ball. What the hell is that all about? You drop Roger Ebert and a Raisinet and they hit the ground at the same time? Bullshit.

Kelvin, metric, inertia—if you can't smoke it, it's not real and it's certainly no concern of Peter Greene's or the other clutch actors with the less catchy names. If only Sir Isaac Newton were here to have this cookie bonk him in the noggin. Who knows what he might have found?

Probably a pure interpersonal dynamic, splitting action, and Scorcese-like realism. Jean de Segonzac's hand-held cam yanks you onto the streets and keeps you there for the duration. Quality.

1991 (100 min.). Peter Greene, Edie Falco, Adam Trese. Dir.: Nick Gomez.

    𝔇   𝒱𝓛

Let's Get Lost

Documentary/biography of fifties musician Chet Baker.

There's a time and a place for everything. Somethings, there are more times and places for, like eating chips and salsa or smoking pot, as offhand examples. The rest of the time is generally reserved for entertainment, and during this time, during the subset of this time when you are in the mood for a mellow, kind of hazy, take-you-to-another-world, black-and-white, very cool, musical, documentary, semifascinating, partially intellectual kind of blue-ice, opium experience, this is what you want.

We realize this mood doesn't happen every day, but neither does Chet Baker. The guy was a fifties trumpet player/singer, for your information, and he had a voice that can only be characterized as straddling that line between a low woman's voice and a high man's voice. If you closed your eyes and listened, you honestly couldn't tell. He sung these really surreal tunes and played trumpet in generally the same way.

Something about being high and Chet Baker is a natural match. Add photographer/filmmaker Bruce Weber to the mix and you've got more than a natural match. You've got an unsung hero that can sing.

1989 (119 min.). Chet Baker. Dir.: Bruce Weber.

        𝔽

Local Hero

A young American executive's comic struggles to bring an oil refinery to a Scottish coastal village populated with—you guessed it—eccentric Scottish people.

The little things. The simple beauties that make everyday life so enjoyable. They're not spectacular, but they bring oodles of happiness. And they always deliver. Like the shake at the bottom of a cafeteria ice cream cone. The finster in the back pocket of the jeans you haven't worn in months. Watching small children run very fast, lose control, fall on the ground, skin their knee, and begin to cry. The tiny little tea leaves of Tetley tea. A fully packed bowl that someone forgot to smoke. Masturbation.

And *Local Hero*. It had the "quirky" little town with the "quirky" locals well before Cicely, Rome, and Twin Peaks introduced this once respectable adjective to national prominence and finally overexposure. Toss in the always reliable Burt Lancaster, with just a hint of mermaids, and your evening is taken care of.

It'll never blow your mind. But you'll always leave it feeling good. Feeling happy. We can all use a little of that.

1983 (111 min.). Peter Riegert, Burt Lancaster, Denis Lawson, Jenny Seagrove. Dir.: Bill Forsyth.

The Maltese Falcon 🌿 🌿 🌿 🌿

After the mysterious death of his partner, PI Sam Spade must fight off thieves, murderers, and a beautiful woman in a quest for a priceless statue.

Don't bother concentrating too much on the plot; all you need to know is that it's Bogey, and there's some kind of treasure hunt going on.

You're lucky if you understand what the hell the actors are talking about. And therein lies the key. This adaptation of Dashiell Hammett's potboiler is classic film noir, a genre of movies where all the characters are secretly hitting a bong behind the scenes. The primary example of covert pot smoking by a *Maltese Falcon* character is that of Guttman, the sinister and corpulent mastermind behind the quest. Tell us if these aren't the words of a baked individual:

> I distrust a closemouthed man. He generally picks the wrong time to talk and says the wrong things. Talking's something you can't do judiciously, unless you keep in practice. Now, sir, we'll talk if you like. I'll tell you right out, I'm a man who likes talking to a man who likes to talk.

We rest our case.

1941 (100 min.). Humphrey Bogart, Mary Astor, Peter Lorre, Sydney Greenstreet. Dir.: John Huston.

    VL   VS

Mindwalk: A Film for Passionate Thinkers

A conversation among a politician, a poet, and a scientist.

Something about growing systems and a lake.

1991 (110 min.). Liv Ullmann, Sam Waterston, John Heard, Ione Skye. Mus.: Philip Glass. Dir.: Bernt Capra.

    D   VL

The Name of the Rose

Friar Tuck meets Rockford.

The most baffling mystery of our time is not why monks are dying in *The Name of the Rose*. It's not the success of *Dirty Dancing*. It's Radio Shack.

This is the lamest, most rinky-dink crap known to man, but somehow, they're everywhere. Sure, people need remote-control cars and phone jacks, but what the hell? The ratio of Radio Shacks to the populace has escalated to 2:1. For every one person there are now at least two Radio Shacks.

Combine clergy with Connery with cryptic book with cannabis and you're still no closer to a quality metal detector. Fourteenth-century monks are dropping like Realistic clarity levels, and no one can figure it out. Bond-turned-priest heads for abbey and digs into quagmire. It's almost as confounding as Wesley Snipes, but a lot less stilted.

Secret doors and portals, ornate books and ancient curses, hints of magic, nothing conclusive on who the hell buys those Tandy robots, but enough cool mysticism to spark your bowl.

1986 (130 min.). Sean Connery, F. Murray Abraham, Christian Slater, William Hickey. Dir.: Jean-Jacques Annaud.

  VS

The Navigator: A Medieval Odyssey 🌿 🌿 🌿 🌿

Supernaturally gifted fourteenth-century child leads plague-threatened people through earth into modern New Zealand.

Didn't you always want time-travel powers? You could've stopped *Turk 182!* Warned everyone about Keanu Reeves. Helped Kareem manage his assets. Bought arcade-size video games for your newlywed parents. Started a pro-life pizza chain. Assisted George Washington Carver when he did something with peanuts or something. When Ronald Reagan was shot, you could have warned Brady.

The Navigator has a more serious agenda. A completely unusual and atypical picture with ripping cinematography and uncommon emotion. Unfamiliar in almost every regard. An unsung hero if there ever was.

1988 (92 min.). Hamish McFarlane, Bruce Lyons, Chris Haywood. Dir.: Vincent Ward.

1983 NCAA Final Four Semifinal 🌿 🌿 🌿 🌿

Louisville vs. Houston.

Don't settle for the official NCAA highlight film, which shows the whole game in slow motion. Do whatever it takes to get your hands on a tape of the actual contest. This is not a suggestion simply for hoops fans. Anyone can appreciate the unbelievable athleticism and sheer basketball artistry that these two teams showed in one classic contest. Considered the dunkathon of all ages, this game featured more slams than a Hüsker

Dü show as the Houston Cougars of Clyde the Glide and Akeem the Dream pounded the Cardinals into submission. Lost amongst the famed members of Phi Slamma Jamma, watch for little-known and long-forgotten Benny Anders to provide you with the most spectacular display. No other sporting event comes this close to giving you exactly what you want out of a high: instant gratification.

1983 (approx. 100 min.). CBS Sports.

Paris, Texas

1983 Palme d'or winner at Cannes. Hypnotic Sam Shepard interlude about missing father who suddenly reappears and reunites with son.

Paris, Texas is like taking a shit. There's some rocky moments in there, it takes a little longer than you'd like, but when it's over, you're happy you did it and you have something intelligent to talk about. Hence, this one's for our more literate Potatoes. The completely braindead and associate brain-dead should please proceed to *The Cannonball Run.*

Now that no one's reading, Harry Dean Stanton doesn't talk for the first twenty minutes. Have no fear, Dean Stockwell, the music, and the visuals are more than enough. The music particularly. Slow-paced, slow-building molasses tension, to the eventual confrontation with the boy's mother, Nastassja Kinski. Good for a postapocalyptic evening at the lake when all of humanity is dead and you have no commitments.

1984 (150 min.). Harry Dean Stanton, Nastassja Kinski, Dean Stockwell, Hunter Carson, Aurore Clement. Dir.: Wim Wenders.

The Power of Myth

Baked guy in regular chair figures out universe.

Six-tape series of writer/philosopher Joseph Campbell as interviewed by Bill Moyers. It's kind of a shame because you can tell Moyers had no clue what was really going on. Sounds like Ronald Reagan again? It's not his fault. Joseph Campbell was a full fourth-tier genius: Hendrix, the guys who wrote the Bible, those grease trucks that sell gyros, and Joseph Campbell, in that order.

You may find this hidden gem at your library. It's quite the PBS, literary type of thing. Now that doesn't mean you need a Channel 13 umbrella to appreciate. It just means you don't want to call up friends and be like, "Duderonomy, I got a monster bag of the super-killer kind. I got the *Bloodsport* and the Joseph Campbell. Van Dammage and a little theology, bra? What you say?"

Just say no. Religion, perspective, myth, the basis of *Star Wars,* everything seems to make sense within Campbell's system of beliefs.

There's a time and a place. Usually you get fries. Sometimes, at a nice restaurant, you opt for something a little healthier and more sophisticated.

Series includes:
Tape 1: *"Hero's Adventure."*
Tape 2: *"Message of Myth."*
Tape 3: *"First Storytellers."*
Tape 4: *"Sacrifice and Bliss."*
Tape 5: *"Love and Goddess."*
Tape 6: *"Masks of Eternity."*

1988.

     F

Runaway Train 🌿 🌿 🌿 🌿

Brain-surgeon convicts escape from prison aboard train hurtling toward derailment in northern Canada.

Something about public transportation makes you nervous. It's part the public, part the transportation. Why do you have to stow your bags securely under the seat in front of you? Gimme some of those salted peanuts and beat it. If the plane's going down, we're all dead. With or without leg room.

Ever wish you could save the plane from hijackers or jump out ten feet before it crashes and roll like a good *Fall Guy* episode to innocuous and predictable safety? Why do you die if you jump up right before an elevator hits bottom?

Well, *Runaway Train* won't solve mysteries better left to the guys who build the exploding space shuttle, but it will rivet you pretty hard for an unsung hero. Tense locomotion, gray and gritty, sort of like Prague but without those vile sausages.

 Based on a screenplay by Akira Kurosawa.

1985 (111 min.). Jon Voight, Eric Roberts, Rebecca DeMornay. Dir.: Andrei Konchalovsky.

 VS

The Seventh Voyage of Sinbad 🌿 🌿 🌿 🌿

That famous Arabian sailor's greatest, most harrowing adventure.

You know where the evening is headed. A bunch of people crowding into the room, passing the bong in a rapidly widening circle, and listening to tunes loud enough that you can't hear the person next to you. At least three people will be endlessly bobbing their heads to the beat, lost in the subtleties and textures of the music. For those of you with your eyes open, it's nice to have something to watch on the tube. Something that you don't have to hear to follow. Something that will please your eyes and soothe your mind.

The man who executes the game plan to the coach's greatest satisfaction? The captain, who, on this or any of his Ray Harryhausen–school of stop-motion animated voyages, always comes through in the clutch. You don't need sound to watch most of Sinbad's buddies get chowed down by one horrible monster after another. The stuff you loved as a kid is even better when you're putting your head in a different kind of childlike state. He always pulls it out in the end, guts the bad guy, gets the girl, the treasure, and the kingdom back, and leaves a trail of cyclopean corpses behind.

Listen to the music. Hit the mute button. And enjoy the sensory overload.

1958 (87 min.). Kerwin Mathews, Kathryn Grant, Richard Eyer. Dir.: Nathan Juran.

Skillz to Pay the Billz

A compilation of popular and rarely seen videos of the Beastie Boys.

There is that stage, however brief, that we all go through. It was a pleasant time to be alive, so let's go back there for a moment. Right about the time we first began to get baked, when everything was new and exciting. Remember? There were lots of uncontrollable laugh attacks. Late-night binges at the chili dog/nacho stand were the norm. Paranoia, bad trips, and the DEA never crossed the mind. And every movie, video, or TV show was filled with subtle messages that could only be discovered if you were high. Hell, everyone who produced this media had to be high as well, or else how could they just . . . know? It's all coming back now, isn't it?

But as time went by, and pot was smoked, you were hit with an unpleasant revelation. It was sort of like the day you realized the pilgrims didn't share a happy Thanksgiving Day turkey with the Native Americans, but instead robbed them of their homes and dignity. You were forced to accept the fact that the world of entertainment didn't completely revolve around marijuana. It only seemed that way. Wasn't the happiest of moments, was it?

Ah, but *Skillz to Pay the Billz* reminds us of how it used to be. Relive those days of blissful ignorance with the absolute assurance that every second was geared specifically for the naive pot-fiend that exists in all of us. By far, the best of its kind.

Can only be ordered directly from the Beastie Boys merchandising company, Grand Royal. P.O. Box 26689, Los Angeles, CA 90026.

1992 (40 min.). The King Ad-Rock, MCA, Mike D. Various directors.

Story of Ricky

Ricky, the greatest fighter that ever lived, and master of "breath control," wreaks unparalleled (and we mean unparalleled) havoc on corrupt prison community.

There are two types of people in this world: people who have experienced *Story of Ricky* and people who haven't.

After three hours of contemplating this review, all we can say is that no human being could ever accurately depict the contents of *Story of Ricky* in words. *Story of Ricky* is utterly and completely mind-boggling. *Story of Ricky* is fucking absurd.

Required: a lot of pot. Decent- to large-size, semianimated group. A lot of pot. *Veterans only.*

In Chinese with English subtitles.
P.S. The guy with the deformed head—it's his hair.

1991 (90 min.). Fan Siu Wang, Ukari Oshima, Kuo Chui, Gloria Yip, Frankie Chan. Dir.: Lan Nai Kai.

Superfly

Coke dealer gone good, looks for one last shipment before leaving "the life."

The car alone is worth the price of admission. Then add the music and you're making money. Then add the super-stylin', leather-suit-wearin', mutton-chop-sportin', joint-smokin', ankh-necklaced, coke-sniffin' savvy man himself. Now you've got a portfolio worth discussing.

Before you leave your hovel, dump your friends and hit the pork-belly market, roast up for a righteous seventies flashback, a sacred visit to the decade that paid homage to the stoner. And *Superfly* is no exception. Note the full five-to-seven minute "pusher man" montage surrounded by the Curtis Mayfield experience. *Superfly* had respect for our kind.

Did we mention the car? The clothes? The intangible magic that seventies filmmaking always exudes?

Yes, we did. But we're not afraid to say it again, because after all, there's clearly no rhyme or reason to what the hell we're talking about half the time. This goes for *Superfly* as well. It isn't what's said, it's how it feels. And baby, it feels good.

1972 (96 min.). Ron O'Neal, Carl Lee, Sheila Frazier, Julius W. Harris. Dir.: Gordon Parks Jr.

Swimming to Cambodia

Spalding Gray recounts his experiences during the shooting of The Killing Fields.

You're off your game. That's clear to everyone involved. You can't seem to get a word in edgewise, and when you do, it's not pretty. You're thinking faster than you can talk, finishing sentences in your head, making no sense at all. Strange. Last night, you held the room in your pot-stained fingertips, regaling it with tales both humorous and wise. Tonight, the group dynamic is floundering; everybody waits for someone else to pick up the ball, for someone else to steer the verbal tiller with a confident, steady hand. If only you could say something funny. Something coherent. Anything.

Let it go. For one evening, allow Spalding Gray to be your guide. Your conversational Sherpa, if you will. The room will go quiet as everyone is captured by the world's greatest monologuist's stories of drugs, decadence, and evil on the set of Roland Joffe's classic true-life epic. Don't attempt to figure out why no one seems to understand you, or want to hear what you have to say. At least for the next hour and a half, the pressure's off.

1987 (87 min.). Spalding Gray. Dir.: Jonathan Demme.

  F

The Towering Inferno, The Poseidon Adventure, Airport '77, and anything made by Irwin Allen 🌿 🌿 🌿

A bunch of fading stars are thrown together in one contrived setting and systematically tortured by a cruel twist of Mother Nature's fickle hand of fate.

Watch one and you've seen them all. A large group of people gather in a building or mode of transport, most likely something revolutionary in design yet structurally unsound. A low-ranking member of the organization in charge of safety points out that it's too dangerous to have a gathering of this size, but his or her greedy, arrogant superior cuts corners and disregards the warning. Of course, the prediction of doom is accurate, and initial deaths are plentiful and graphic. A small, feisty group of survivors must somehow stay alive in the face of outlandish odds. They consist of a quiet, humble yet crafty leader, a beautiful love interest, a small child, and an elderly superstar from Hollywood's golden age who dies painfully after an astonishing act of personal courage. Don't forget the asshole who always contradicts the leader, demands they go the other way, and leads a secondary group of malcontents to a horribly violent yet somehow satisfying death. If the survivors are lucky, an outside force brings in a bad-ass expert in rescue operations to save the day. Before the film ends, one of your favorite characters, usually the black guy, dies, giving it a nice, melancholic aftertaste. Predictable? Maybe. But they deliver with a consistency only the Simpson family (Homer's, not Orenthal James's) can match.

P.S. Rent only as the fifth movie in a five-flix-for-five-nights-for-five-dollars special. They do poorly under pressure.

 VS

The Trials of Life: Hunting and Escaping 🌿 🌿 🌿 🌿

Does the Discovery Channel know all its viewers are stoned?

There's randomness for the sake of randomness and randomness that delivers. Having an eighties party is the former. Our suggestion that you seek out this video is the latter.

The opening bird sequence will blow you away.

The killer whale sequence will blow you away.

Test your loyalties as Shamu storms the beach to assault the fuzzy sea lions. Learn the equation of true horror as a band of cute little chimps do unspeakable things to a colobus monkey. And ants . . . not just any ants, but African army ants, the kind that nothing in the world can stop, the kind that every animal in the jungle runs in terror from. The perfect social system. Their only purpose? To move forward, crushing, killing, and destroying everything in their path, just for the glory of the queen. Something about her drives them to go on a mad, murderous quest to honor her. Nothing stops them, not rivers, not lions, not people . . . nothing. Now, if some derivative, schlock garage band can get people to smash each other to bits, think about what the ants are listening to . . .

Must-see.

Kudos to Time-Life for producing something of substance. Time-Life Video: 1-800-621-7026.

1991 (60 min.). Written and hosted by David Attenborough.

      H

12:01 🌿 🌿 🌿 🌿

A man is eternally trapped in a moment in time.

Somewhere it had to be said. Somewhere is here. While everyone heaped praise upon *Groundhog Day* for its inventive plot, the short film it ripped off was left in the cold. One hour repeats itself forever, and that guy who always plays assholes (dad from *Dead Poets Society*, evil DA in *True Believer*), is actually a sympathetic figure as he tries to escape eternity's grasp. Based on the short story by Richard Lupoff, the permutations are endless; the film would've been much better received had they simply called it *Mind-fuck*. Part comedy, part tragic love story, and all sci-fi thriller, make 12:01 P.M. your favorite time of day, immediately following 4:20.

> Beware: There is also an extended TV movie bearing the same name, starring Jonathan Silverman. Be careful to get the short version.

1990 (?). Kurtwood Smith.

             �

The Uninvited 🌿 🌿 🌿

A cruise ship populated by college kids and a morose George Kennedy is terrorized by what looks suspiciously like a possessed feline.

The USA network. Have you ever wondered how this purveyor of bad television has managed to stay afloat? It airs nothing but cartoons that even kids hate to watch (that German anteater guy, for instance), teen sex comedies with all the nude scenes cut out, and slasher flicks without the payoff of multiple decapitations. Maybe an occasional made-for-TV movie starring the last three actors to escape from the Betty Ford Clinic.

But there is one inescapable fact that ensures USA's place on every pot smoker's recall button: At any time of any day, turn it on and see something you've never seen before. Most likely never wanted to and won't want to now, but the opportunity always exists for something to leap from the refuse heap like so many demon cats shedding their false coverings of soft, orange fur.

Hence, this darkest of thoroughbreds. Never, *never* pay money for it. But if you're lucky enough to stumble upon it while enjoying a late-night strafing run, call your buddies, a reliable source, and Burrito Palace. Consider yourself *Uninvited*.

1988 (89 min.). Alex Cord, George Kennedy, Toni Hudson. Dir.: Greydon Clark.

The Vanishing (original version) ☘ ☘ ☘ ☘

A man desperately searches for his missing girlfriend.

To an audience grown numb from watching the local news, as well as the countless bad horror flicks of the eighties, a truly horrific moment of filmmaking is a rare thing indeed. About as rare as a rerun of the cartoon that showed Chewbacca on his home planet, and just as coveted by the true cannabacinephile. This is what *The Vanishing* provides in spades. Instead of going for cheap shock-scares or gore (which certainly have their places in the world), it builds up a slow, steady, unbearable tension. This is not normally what we're seeking when the potatoes are in the oven, but consider this. If you knew the existence of a substance that gave you a two-hour-long happy buzz that slightly increased its intensity with each passing minute, then culminated in a moment of such astonishing power and clarity that you'd probably never experienced anything like it before, would you give it a try? Even if you knew there might be a little fear that came along for the ride? The climax of *The Vanishing* is the instant when it all kicks in. It's not all that pleasant, but it's new. Newness. Remember that?

Care to sample?

> *Pointless to see more than once, unless you're with your mother.*

1988 (101 min.). Bernard-Pierre Donnadieu, Gene Bervoets, Johanna Ter Steege. Dir.: George Sluizer.

Vanishing Point 🌿 🌿 🌿

A deranged Vietnam vet takes a dare from his speed pusher to make it from Denver to San Francisco in fifteen hours...

Hasn't that happened to all Baked Potatoes on the way to satisfying that certain craving? The supplier is always questioning your conviction, testing you, making you prove yourself even though you've already earned your stripes time and time again. Get on the road, then . . . fuck the speed limit, the hitchhikers, the cops . . . especially fuck the cops. Drive till there are no more laws to break and no more road to drive. And when you hit the ocean, don't turn around like that gutless, witless moron, Gump. Grind your molars to the bloody gums and plunge over the edge with that shit-eating, speed-beating grin on your face. Yeah. *Yeah!!!!!!!!!!!!!!!!!!!*

Then watch the hacks steal your movie, put two women at the wheel, and call it a refreshing exercise in feminist role reversal. Forget *Thelma & Louise*. We've got Kowalski and the white Supercharger. We've got the granddaddy of 'em all. We've got *Vanishing Point!*

1971 (107 min.). Barry Newman, Cleavon Little, Dean Jagger. Dir.: Richard C. Sarafian.

Whiskey 🌿 🌿 🌿 🌿

*A visceral, troubling, funny-as-shit glance into the cycles of
violence, urban chaos, and abuse that permeate our besieged
and embattled skate- and snowboarding youth.*

What's wrong with the kids these days? If we could only sit down each
little youngster and say, "Little youngster, it's OK to be a scumbag, a hate
monger, a Nazi Youth organizer, just don't do drugs. Drugs will make
you into a giant salamander." If we could just rid the world of Satan's
candy it would all be OK.

You see, America's future lies in its youth. And that's not a good thing.
But take heart. If there was any hope, even a glimmer, *Whiskey* banishes
it forever.

The future is but a black hole vortex where we will all be crushed like
imploding atomic waffles.

Carpe diem! Let's follow heavily disturbed snow- and skateboarders in
their quest to smash whiskey bottles over their own heads. A genius plot
thread indeed, intertwined with skate- and snowboard footage, altercations with society, and then fermented into *Whiskey*, a truly deranged
glimpse of malfunctioning humanity.

In the genteel words of BPAC Chairman Ted Pryde: "Could have done
without the dog with the stiffee." To each his own.

Offensive but charming. Thirty-two minutes. The perfect appetizer.

*199? (32 min.). Herman Kahz, Steve Kearns, Ralph Boyce, Barry Walsh,
Moses Itkonen, Sean Johnson, Jimmy Halopoff, Colin McKay, Kevin
Young, Mike Hager, Sid n Judah, Kris Markovich. Boozy the Clown Productions/Gush Clothing.*

       H

Wicked City

A futuristic earth where humans attempt to establish peaceful relations with a race of other-dimensional aliens that share the same plane of reality.

There are those movies that can fully entertain a roomful of people. Any people. There are also those that will cause the same people to sob in boredom. And then there are films that fall somewhere in between— films that will, over the course of their time on-screen, weed out certain members of the group for different reasons and leave a chosen few to enjoy the fade to black. *Wicked City,* animated by the same wizards that brought you *Akira,* is just such an in-betweener.

Throughout the film's one and a half hours, viewers shall excuse themselves for a number of reasons: squeamishness over the best kind of excessively graphic violence, fatigue due to certain scenes that explore the unbearable slowness of being, castration anxiety, the unbelievably misogynistic script, confusion over just what the hell is happening. The following is a brief description of those who will stick it out.

All three are male. One is a lifelong collector of comic books who can't even enjoy the film due to feeling somehow responsible for the fact that everyone else crashed. The second is someone who smokes pot in an almost medicinal manner and enjoys whatever's on-screen for him to watch, including static. The third's reason for continuing is simply to establish the fact that he can stay up later than everyone else, therefore claiming some bizarre sense of victory. They are each too stoned to speak.

If any of these men are you, *Wicked City* is the town for you.

1992 (90 min.). Dir.: Yoshiaki Kawajiri.

Wings of Desire 🌿 🌿 🌿 🌿

The life and times of angels in Berlin. And Columbo.

At last, Wim Wenders stopped toying with our heads and boring us to tears. The legendary German auteur has finally put all his talents into one near-perfect movie. *Wings of Desire* is a long, incredibly beautiful experience that demands that you focus your thoughts into a peaceful, iambic rhythm in order to remain conscious. It won't be easy, but the best things rarely are. It's like the phone conversation with your grandmother right after you've pulled the three-foot tube. Dicey at first, but once you get the hang of it, you're rewarded with a positive, life-affirming experience. Especially when granny sends you the three-hundred-dollar care package because you let that bit about the munchies slip.

Wings of Desire will unquestionably do you right, but there is one warning we do feel compelled to offer: Try not to be unnerved by the idea that your thoughts might not be *your* thoughts, but simply the whispered suggestions of invisible forces from a higher plane who are leaning over your shoulder this very moment. Watching you. Always.

1988 (130 min.). Bruno Ganz, Solveig Dommartin, Otto Sander, Curt Bois, Peter Falk. Dir.: Wim Wenders.

    VS

GUEST REVIEW

Reviewer:
Donal Logue
Occupation:
Actor (MTV Cab Driver Guy, And the Band Played On, Diabolique,
The Grave)

Withnail & I 🌿 🌿 🌿 🌿

Read the review.

I am not stoned as I write this, though the people at this hotel are wary of me and wonder why I constantly call at all hours for coffee to be brought to my room, where the smoke hangs in ominous, stinky clouds. It's not that I don't tip well, it's more likely they're frightened of the underwear I choose to wear, underwear which I purchase by the tube. They suspect I'm a drugie and that my friends are prostitutes. Not that this has anything to do with whether I'm stoned or not, it's just that I've lost my sense of smell. I'm convinced that the message light on my phone is blinking. I see flashes of orange in my peripheral vision, but when I turn to look, it is just a dark piece of reflective orange plastic. Interesting. I like to enhance the quality of bad pot with angel dust.

I first saw posters for *Withnail & I* in London in January of 1989. Ralph Steadman had done the artwork, so I naturally wrote the movie off as some kind of British, junior-varsity version of the already questionable work of Hunter S. Thompson. To equate Steadman with Thompson, however, may be an injustice equal to linking Hesse with the already Tolkien-poisoned American hippies who took the great German writer to heart during the summer of love (Phillips Exeter Academy, 1986).

My girlfriend convinced me to see the film. We had scored some good dope through a Dutch exchange student at Regent's College named Mark, who I discovered later had an uncircumsized penis, a fact salient to this story, though I can't remember why. The girl (also uncircumsized) ultimately left me for a banker, but that's not important. What is, is that I went to Harvard and he didn't and that while extremely baked when we saw the film, we nonetheless had the wits about us to recognize a work of genius. It is a love story between a modern-day Hamlet, Withnail, and his unsuspecting roommate, I. While it starts on the sophomoric level of other films romanticizing excessive poverty and drug use in late-sixties London (see *Goodbye, Mr. Chips),* it develops into a confusingly wonderful tale of unrequited love on the part of English public school homosexuals whose brilliant cynicism, while providing some witty comedy, unfortunately also brought about eighties English synth-pop bands and the ultimate ruin of English culture (see *Maurice).*

This historical truism is evident on a number of levels in the film. For instance, the pain of Uncle Monty's decision to give up the boards, when he awoke and "quite reasonably said to myself, I shall never play the Dane," and his inability to seduce I, reflect England's desire to be Denmark and the military impossibility of its ever doing so. Furthermore, the subtlety of the film's own brand of anti-Semitism screams *the Dreyfus Affair,* and the triumphant conclusion, when our protagonist completely fucks up Hamlet's soliloquy from Shakespeare in which he reveals to Rosencrantz and Guildenstern that "This goodly frame, the earth" and all its inhabitants "delights me not," all summed, creates a cinematic allegorical soup that will warm the tummies of scholars of English history for many years to come, dry nights or warm (bud-wise). I'm

Irish and it's good to see an English film cut right to the core of why the English Empire folded not long after the Battle of Britain.

My phone is blinking. I am not stoned as I write this; I am only waiting for my coffee.

1987 (105 min.). Richard E. Grant, Paul McGann, Richard Griffiths, Ralph Brown, Michael Elphick. Dir.: Bruce Robinson.

VL

BAKED POTATOES

DEA
600/700 Army Navy Drive
Arlington, VA 22202
Attn.: Demand Reduction

Dear Demand Reduction:

We're writing to you as a last recourse. A number of our friends have purchased this newly released book. Supposedly it's a treatise recommending various films to watch during a marijuana-influenced viewing.

Of course pot is no big deal when you look at the scope of the problem, and we've all seen that enforcement is completely pointless in terms of curbing drug use, but our situation is a bit more mundane. These alleged "friends" of ours who are now more like vegetables have begun spending all of their time within the gripping pages of the text. We're afraid to even look at it lest we get addicted to the poison.

Now, of course, we all believe in a person's right to do whatever they wish as long as it doesn't infringe on the rights of others, but we feel that this text is taking away our friends, thereby constituting infringement. All they do is smoke pot, consult the text, and rent movies. They eat constantly and have begun to express unpatriotic, cynical views on the world. We're afraid they might be communists, or worse. We don't want them to get in trouble, just to get help. Is there something that can be done? Do you know of any national hotlines they can call for help? What can you do when someone essentially mutates into a Baked Potato? Is it unhealthy or just a phase?

Looking forward to your advice:

Jim and Pakky Bole

U.S. DEPARTMENT OF JUSTICE

DRUG ENFORCEMENT ADMINISTRATION

Washington, D.C. 20537

February 9, 1995

Jim and Pakky Bole
418 Richard Place
Ithaca, New York 14850

Dear Jim and Pakky Bole:

Thank you for your recent letter requesting assistance in helping to solve your friends' drug problems.

It is assumed from the tone of your letter that your friends are adult and therefore, have reached the age of reason, that is, they have attained the capability to choose between what is right and what is wrong. No one has forced their decisions on them.

Sit down with your friends, discuss with them what you see and how you feel about their behavior, and suggest that they have a problem which requires expert guidance. Offer to help them find help. There are numerous local hot lines listed in the telephone directory, and even the local emergency room could provide this information.

However, people with problems cannot be helped until they first acknowledge they have a problem, and also desire to be helped. So, if your friends rebuff your offers now, they may eventually decide you were right and seek help sometime in the future. In the meantime, don't follow in their footsteps, and find yourselves some new friends.

Sincerely,

Ronald J. Trethric
Chief
Demand Reduction Section

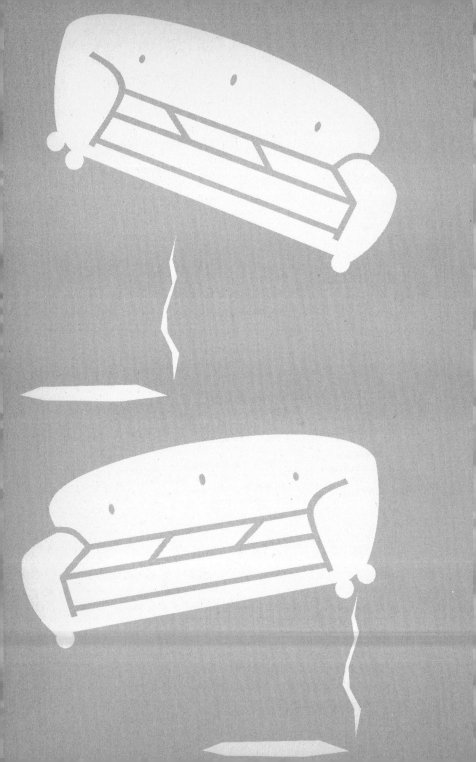

IV.
Risky Calls

The risky calls can be precarious territory. On the right day, when Saturn is aligned with Mercury and the Pharisees play pinball in Gibraltar, a Brazil or The Fly provides a positive, uplifting, BP experience. On the wrong day, however, it can land a devastating blow, dismantling weeks of expensive, self-perpetuating psychotherapy and spiraling the innocent traveler toward a renewed marijuana dependency.

Ah, the age-old lesson. Events that seem negative at first do, in retrospect, lead to constructive results. Behold, the spirit of the risky call.

After Hours

Everything can and does go wrong in a nightmare excursion into the East Village.

There are those that call *After Hours* a delightfully twisted black comedy. And in certain controlled situations, this might be true. Viewed behind the door clubs and motion sensors of your parents' suburban fortress, dead sober, you'll certainly enjoy Martin Scorsese's edgy exploration of Murphy's Law in Manhattan. But stoned? Do you really want to experience a lifetime of the wired, oppressive stress that only New York can conjure, distilled into ninety-seven anxiety-ridden minutes. Sound like fun? Yeah, maybe in that speed-laced-acid, grind-your-teeth-to-the-gums-and-claw-your-own-eyes-out sort of way. In your or a friend's apartment, with the nature of your buzz teetering in the balance, it's not simply a risky call. It's a bad one.

1985 (97 min.). Griffin Dunne, Rosanna Arquette, Linda Fiorentino, John Heard, Teri Garr, Cheech and Chong, Bronson Pinchot. Dir.: Martin Scorsese.

  D VL

Akira

The plot is unintelligible and unimportant. Suffice it to say that "Neo-Tokyo" is about to explode!

The first thing that needs to be stated is that there's no way any normal human makes it past the first forty minutes of the confused story line, unless you're being administered a healthy dose of Droog Aversion Therapy. That said, the first half hour offers you a glimpse of what might've been. Unquestionably, it is the greatest animation ever put on film. It's not enough to carry the day, but will get it off to a good start.

To maximize enjoyment, use this simple but effective technique: After the thirty-minute mark, begin to fast-forward the tape until you see someone or something explode. Rewind to the beginning of the scene, and consume. This will come in handy at least seven to eight times, and will transform a seemingly endless exercise in cartoon onanism into a ripping forty-seven-minute short film . . . what *Akira* was always meant to be.

1988 (124 min.). Dir.: Katsuhiro Otomo.

Barnyard Frenzy

Find it and see.

Blue Velvet

Norman Rockwell gone very, very bad.

We all loved our hometown. We loved its secure, tree-lined streets and the childhood memories they invoked. We treasured the local lore and the characters who continue to foster it as we speak. The high school . . . the park . . . that place where your first kiss fell on you like a gift from on high. Like the Boss said, this your 'ometown.

And then David Lynch came along, waving his ear, and ruined everything. He had to rip the cover off, expose the seedy underbelly of the American myth of suburban peace and happiness. Diamond Dave forced us to take a long look at what skulked behind the drawn curtains and dimmed lights of all those picket fences. And this is what we found: The Little League coach you idolized had been molesting his players after practice. Your favorite English teacher was having an affair with a fourteen-year-old student. The unique multicultural makeup of the town was a sham—the Jews hated the blacks who hated them right back, the Italians hated them both, the white trash hated everyone, especially themselves. The respected town elders were lifelong alcoholics. And you were a dysfunctional pot smoker.

This is a great movie. But remember one very important thing before you make this most dicey of calls: Ignorance is . . . well, you know.

1986 (120 min.). Kyle MacLachlan, Isabella Rossellini, Dennis Hopper, Laura Dern, Dean Stockwell, Hope Lange, Brad Dourif. Dir.: David Lynch.

☠ ⊕ ♪   VS

Brazil

A dystopian view of the future seen through the eyes of a civil servant who is crushed by the system for which he works.

Yes, *Brazil* is directed by the same Terry Gilliam of *Time Bandits* and *Monty Python* fame. Yes, it contains all the same trippy effects and nutty characters. But watching this flick stoned is like being lost at the back end of Bourbon Street during Mardi Gras on two hits of acid. Trippy effects. Nutty characters. No fun at all.

The viewer spends 131 oppressive minutes being reminded that the common man is nothing but a cog in the corporate wheel . . . powerless and expendable. The inevitable results of the experience? If you're still in school, you'll find a way to make that six-year plan economically feasible for your parents. If you're a nine-to-fiver, you'll be on the phone with your therapist before you reach the halfway point. You're better off renting a two-hour compilation of your botched job interviews.

Let the intelligentsia call this a scathing Orwellian satire. We won't be there to talk you down.

1985 (131 min.). Jonathan Pryce, Kim Greist, Robert De Niro, Katherine Helmond, Ian Holm, Bob Hoskins, Michael Palin, Ian Richardson. Dir.: Terry Gilliam.

The Cannonball Run

"You can never go hungry underestimating the tastes of the American public."

Sometimes when you watch *The Cannonball Run* you feel like there was this one giant trailer in which all the actors were hanging out doing lines with Dom DeLuise, and some production assistant knocked on the door every now and then and dragged a few people out to do a scene.

It's old-fashioned eighties moviemaking, but it works. Burt Reynolds and The Dom (DeLuise) masquerade as paramedics, elude el piggies, traverse nation in cross-country quest. Lest you forget: the cars, the panache, Jamie Farr. Wasn't there a scene when they meet up with Clint and that monkey? Maybe not. Any which way you cut it, *Cannonball* sends you for a somewhat unexpected ride into cultural and cinematic hilarity.

Let's take one last look in that trailer. *Cannonball Run I* and *II:* Burt Reynolds, Dom DeLuise, Dean Martin, Farrah Fawcett, Roger Moore, Adrienne Barbeau, Peter Fonda, Jamie Farr, Marilu Henner, Shirley MacLaine, Jim Nabors, Frank Sinatra, Telly Savalas, Susan Anton, Tim Conway, Sid Caesar, Don Knotts, and Ricardo Montalban.

Jim Nabors. Enough said.

1981 (95 min.). Dir.: Hal Needham.

  VS

Cliffhanger 🍁 🍁 🍁

Diehard in the mountains with no script, no good characters, and Stallone.

There are some who insist that this film falls under the heading of Good Sly. Certainly, there are those that meet this criterion. *Paradise Alley, First Blood, The Lords of Flatbush,* and *Rockys I, II,* and *III* are all eminently watchable, baked or otherwise. But *Cliffhanger* fails to meet the strict standards of this category. The infuriating thing is that we were all duped by the greatest trailer of all time, tricked into spending millions of dollars and reviving Sly's career after *Oscar* and *Stop! or My Mom Will Shoot* died quick, ugly deaths. Now we're not only stuck with Stallone for all eternity, but Renny Harlin is still allowed to make movies. So why does *Cliffhanger* demand inclusion in this compendium?

There are films that are funny because they're supposed to be. Then there are those pretentious bits of celluloid that somehow seem more special; they're not trying to provide comedy, yet that's all they do. There's usually a crux moment in films of this particular ilk; It comes at about the fifteen-minute mark. You can either cling to the futile hope that things will get better, or decide that the movie sucks and delight in each coming failure. The veterans recognize this moment for what it is, and relish it as a rare opportunity for interactive viewing. Consider it the home version of MST3K.

These are a special, treasured breed of movie. And *Cliffhanger* is their king.

1993 (118 min.). Sylvester Stallone, John Lithgow, Michael Rooker, Janine Turner, Paul Winfield, Leon, Max Perlich. Dir.: Renny Harlin.

A Clockwork Orange
🌿 🌿 🌿 🌿

I went to rehab and came back a prairie dog.

When mom and dad sent you to rehab they hadn't seen *A Clockwork Orange* yet. Neither had little Jimmy. You didn't know about your little brother, Jimmy. They had to take you away to the home because you scalded him with that burning bathtub.

But you're all better now. You've duped them into thinking you're cured, but you've only duped yourself, but that's OK.

Enter a disturbing social satire about a sadistic British punk-rocker who rapes and pillages the land of sobriety until he is caught and sent to super-tweaker-futuro rehab hell. This ain't Betty Ford. Here, you've got to be high just to deal with recovery. They pull your eyelids open and make you watch anti-BP propaganda, conditioning you, twisting you, shredding you, till you're no longer even a Baked Potato. You're rice or a choice of vegetable.

Party of three and a bottle of the kind: Malcolm McDowell stars. Stanley Kubrick directs. You watch.

1971 (137 min.). Malcolm McDowell, Patrick Magee, Adrienne Corri. Dir.: Stanley Kubrick.

       $v\mathcal{S}$

Cocksucker Blues

The X-rated rockumentary on the world's greatest rock 'n' roll band.

Not available in video stores as of now. This rarest of gems is worthy of a trip to your local black marketeer. No, it's not always pleasant. You'll probably need to take a hot shower after watching the seedy collection of junkies, groupies, and leeches glom off the band. The decadence of the big time has never been exposed so . . . decadently. There are dicey moments when your desire to wallow in the filth might be pushed to the limit, especially the roadie gang bang on the tour jet with live musical accompaniment by the Stones. But just when you think you've sunk too low to continue, the music brings you back. Mick and the boys jamming with Stevie Wonder or in some dingy bathroom alone is worth the price of admission. Do whatever you can to get your hands on this cult classic. And as a personal aside, avoid looking in the eyes of the junkies . . . you don't need to know what goes on in there.

 Only bootlegged versions of this film are available.

Filmmakers: Robert Frank, Daniel Seymour.

            $\mathcal{H}$

Deliverance 🌿 🌿 🌿

It's so hard to meet people in bars.

There's a part of the United States that people don't always talk about. It's called the South. Remember them? They fought the North in that after-school special. Now, just because your parents are related, that's no reason to avoid *Deliverance*. It's OK to have two heads. More teeth.

What's not OK is getting stuck in the wrong place in the South. Like one of those villages where everyone's wearing white bathrobes and talking about mallards and Reconstruction. You see, that's when "Squeal like a pig, boy," and Ned Beatty pop into your mind. Don't worry. You've got one major thing in your favor: Matlock. If there's any problem, just call Andy, he'll be sure to hop out of the bitter malaise of semiretirement and rescue you from backwoodsmen.

Although he didn't show up to help those four canoers in the film. No one did.

Who cares? You can still get fried and watch it. Not recommended for pre–camping trip family dinners.

P.S. Dueling banjos.

1972 (109 min.). Jon Voight, Burt Reynolds, Ronny Cox, Ned Beatty, James Dickey. Dir.: John Boorman.

    VS

Dolemite 🌿 🌿

Ex-con attempts to settle score with former inmates by assembling gang of kung fu—trained women.

That's a plot you don't see anymore.
The infamous blaxploitation legend. So incredibly bad, it's bad.

1975 (88 min.). Rudy Ray Moore, Jerry Jones. Dir.: D'Urville Martin.

The Exorcist 🌿 🌿 🌿

Uh, she did have a Hardee's cheeseburger.

If there's a little girl who talks like a large beast, vomits, and is living in your attic, chances are she's possessed and needs to be exercised immediately. Not a big deal. Simply pack her a bong hit, prop her up on the Nordictrack, and watch her go. Before you know it, she's shedding the pounds, and Satan along with them.

No need for expensive priests, reverse peristalsis, pasty rotating heads. For just ten easy installments of $10.99, your bile-ridden devil-gnome daughter can be cured as well. But don't call yet. For the next eighty-five seconds, included with Nordictrack, we also offer the revolutionary Soloflex, Multiflex, I'm-Fat-Flex, and the Bonko Steamer. While she works out, you steam your head down to the size of a small macadamia nut. Then stare at the mirror and watch it expand. Ah . . . can't beat the feeling.

Call today and receive *The Exorcist* as your complimentary gift. This Baked Potato classic shows, once and for all, the story of a family's plight when their daughter is possessed by evil spirits. When the film first came out, paramedic teams were needed in the theaters. But no longer!

Don't wait! Call now! 1-900-Fat-Satan. And leave off the *n* for "no clue what this review is about."

> If results not apparent in two weeks, call Franciscan monks and beg.
>
> Based on the bestseller by William Peter Blatty.

1973 (121 min.). Ellen Burstyn, Linda Blair, Jason Miller, Max von Sydow. Dir.: William Friedkin.

  𝒱𝒮

The Fly 🍁 🍁 🍁

Man turns into bug.

No, you're not turning into a fused human-fly, but Jeff Goldblum is. And in ways we never should have seen.

The sequels sure are enticing, though. Get Dan Rather in the machine and combine him with Connie Chung. *Wang Chung.* How bout Larry King mixed with the Michelin Man? Call it *Larry King.*

The only irritating part is that Goldblum gets so close to pulling off that teleportation thing we've been praying for since rush hour on the LIE. So damn close. Like grasping it all, starting to explain it, and

Let's get to the point. *Fly* rhymes with *high,* but don't be fooled. It also rhymes with *I rented* Fly *high and now I have brain sty.* Fine the week you're getting drug tested. Stand clear under normal conditions.

1986 (100 min.). Jeff Goldblum, Geena Davis, John Getz. Dir.: David Cronenberg.

    VS

Ganjasaurus Rex 🍁 🍁

Green piñata turned pot dinosaur emerges from California hills, clubs DEA helicopters, embarrasses filmmakers.

Great name, great idea, and almost funny for a fleeting moment. And then reality hits. Uncle Bud made *G Rex* in a papier-mâché class at the home.

There's a lesson to be learned, however: Think of your movie baked; do not shoot it baked.

For the tasteless, completely incinerated, and elementary school teachers wishing to illustrate the results of severe marijuana dependency.

Nice going-away gift for friends or loved ones off to rehab.

1988 (88 min.). Paul Bassis, Dave Fresh, Rosie Jones. Dir.: Ursi Reynolds.

    Ħ

Heavy Metal

The classic adult comic magazine comes to life in an anthology of animated science fiction tales.

Ask anyone to give you their top twenty-five BP classics, and *Heavy Metal* will invariably slither its way into the mix. Don't be peer-pressured by the pot proletariat's puerile propaganda. A classic case of absence from the video store makes the heart grow fonder. We all liked Journey back in '81, maybe even played the video game, but do you wanna listen to them now? The same goes for this effort from Ivan Reitman's baby-booming bag of tricks, which incidentally includes a fresh tune from Steve Perry and crew on the sound track.

Watch it with anyone who hasn't seen it yet. Start by telling them how great it is. After the first episode dies a slow death, your enthusiasm won't waver. It's the next one that's sweet. The next installment has the amazing animation, remember? The next part has it . . . no . . . no, it doesn't. It's hard, but admitting it is the first step. None of them do, except the final piece. By that time your friends have either fallen asleep or immersed themselves in the Coleco Head-to-Head Football they found tucked under the couch with the "Pac-Man Fever" 45, Pyraminx, and WHERE'S THE BEEF? bumper sticker. Better stuff *Heavy Metal* under there as well. Just another dusty relic from an excessive decade best forgotten.

Heavy Metal is not legally available on video, but it is shown on cable once or twice a year, usually on Cinemax or TBS (edited).

1981 (90 min.). Voices of John Candy, Eugene Levy, Harold Ramis. Dir.: Gerald Potterton.

†

Platoon

War.

They say people decide whether they like a movie about eight to ten minutes in. Now, this is unbaked people. When you're stoned, you can tell in about thirty to sixty seconds if a movie has it. It's an intangible, something subconscious, from the confidence of the camera's first movements you can tell if you're in for a smoker.

From the bell, *Platoon* just rips out of the screen. Charlie Sheen (before you found out he had no standards), Tom Berenger, Willem Dafoe, the eminent Keith David, and Johnny Depp, all on fire in Oliver Stone's definitive Vietnam War saga.

Sure, it's not *Willy Wonka,* but just as a Baked Potato must endure any number and combination of toppings, he or she must also confront the whole spectrum of human emotion and experience. *Platoon* is kind of a bacon-and-cheddar flick. Strong, tasty, fulfilling. You enjoy it but later on you still know you were there.

Risky call but worth the risk.

1986 (120 min.). Charlie Sheen, Willem Dafoe, Tom Berenger, Forest Whitaker, Kevin Dillon, Keith David, Johnny Depp. Dir.: Oliver Stone.

☠ 🔘 🕊 *vs*

Ronald Reagan's 1984 State of the Union Address 🍁 🍁

Everything is not OK.

Watching the *1984 State of the Union Address* is like watching a videotape of yourself when you were five. You keep laughing at it nervously, not believing it actually happened. Then all these strange, old people start smiling and waving at the camera.

If you're wondering whether it's you who's high or the president, take heart, it's probably you. He's just arrestingly clueless. Before you judge the man, though, give him credit where credit is due. He started the War on Drugs, one of the most humorous policies in American history.

Hmmm . . . let's see, it's been sixteen years, billions later, and the "problem" is still getting worse. Should we (a) pretend the war is still working; (b) concentrate more on enforcement; (c) Harass the little guys?

You're right! *D*—all of the above.

This video walks that fine line between the disturbing and the comically absurd—a risky but worthwhile choice.

What were the issues in 1984, anyway?

Don't expect any answers.

      ☊

The Super Bowl 🍁 🍁 🍁 🍁

The technique known as "lip-synching" does not seem to be working.

Baked Potatoes love the Super Bowl. Partially for the fierce human competition. Partially for the pristine synchronized swimmer–like ballet. Partially because rich guys in clown suits chase a bouncing pigskin.

The beauty of the big game, however, lies in its insidious trappings. The debut of every company's earth-shaking ads and products, a startling exercise in deformed cultural estimation. The halftime show complete with middle Americana on parade. Who is middle America anyway? They live in those states that you can't name on a map. They have satellite dishes and eat turkey potpie. They're fed up with gridlock. That's all we know.

The Super Bowl is a risky but exciting call. Before you know it, you're thinking about the apocalypse again. What if Mexico bombed us on Super Bowl Sunday? What if everyone was killed, live, on the highest-rated TV event of the year? Paramedics, trampled screaming babies, carnage. *Faces of Death,* but real.

The Super Bowl high is a gluttonous one. A blitz of visuals, edibles, packed bowls, and insanity. A veritable pot-pourri. And why not? Chaos is your friend.

Taxi Driver

The world according to Travis Bickle.

It all depends on what you're looking for. Uncontrollable laughter? Uh-uh. A pleasant, low-impact happy buzz? Nope. A weighty, introspective, philosophic struggle that compels you to grab pen and paper and figure out what it all means? Dubious. Tripping the light fantastic? We're not quite sure what that means, anyway, but you won't find it here.

How about an electrifying probe into the claustrophobic universe of a rapidly decaying mind locked in a doomed struggle with the seething carnivorous beast that is the Big City that climaxes in a Roman orgy of violence and brutality with no sound except the shallow, cautious breathing of you, the bloodthirsty citizens calling for the heads of Christians?

You want it? Come and get it.

1976 (113 min.). Robert De Niro, Cybill Shepherd, Harvey Keitel, Peter Boyle, Jodie Foster, Albert Brooks, Martin Scorsese. Dir.: Martin Scorsese.

 vs

Twilight Zone—The Movie
 or

The film anthology based on the classic TV series.

If you're lucky, and you forgot everything about this movie, or never saw it or heard anything about it at all, then fast-forward to the final installment of this science fiction collection, directed by *The Road Warrior*'s George Miller. Watch as John Lithgow engages in the greatest battle with an airplane gremlin since the day Bugs got his ass kicked in a cartoon for the first and only time. If this is you, do it now and read no further. (****)

If you don't have the willpower to resist knowing more, then consider this: About three minutes into the initial segment, immediately following the genius opening gambit with Dan Aykroyd and Albert Brooks, you'll be assaulted by the gruesome memory that actor Vic Morrow and two little kids got their heads lopped off by a helicopter while it was filmed. (BS)

Try enjoying the movie now.

1983 (102 min.). Vic Morrow, Scatman Crothers, Kathleen Quinlan, Kevin McCarthy, John Lithgow, Dan Aykroyd, Albert Brooks. Dir.: John Landis, Steven Spielberg, Joe Dante, George Miller.

  vs

2001: A Space Odyssey

I'm sorry Dave, I'm afraid if I hear that Macintosh sound effect again I will put my head in a blender.

2001 is like an Egg McMuffin. Used properly and intelligently, at the right moments and on the right trips, it's a delicacy. Used without proper consideration and timing it's a disgusting mass of lard. The time to call upon a *2001* is, for example, when you're on a ski vacation and everyone goes out to ski and you decide, no way, I wouldn't wake up at 7 A.M. to pull tubes with Franz Klammer.

Everyone leaves, you wake up at noon, and there are ten inches of fresh powder on the ground. You kick yourself, but then you realize, what the hell, I'll get the best of both worlds, I'll go right now. Unfortunately, there's no car at the house. You're screwed.

Wait a minute, there's a truck around back. It's your truck. But where are the keys? You spend three hours looking for the keys. The cat ate the keys and died in the living room. You're screwed again.

Maybe not. *2001* smiles upon you. The phone lines are down, you're on vacation, you tossed the cat in the fireplace, it's the setting for a patient but unequivocal masterpiece. HAL 9000, brilliant story work, great colors and visuals, a few geometric patterns if you look at it right.

Oh, and if you're wondering how you got the movie with no car? The people who own the condo have a stocked fridge, a packed Indian party hookah, and three video tapes: a *MacNeil/Lehrer* special on the Balkans, a Balkan news special on *MacNeil/Lehrer,* and *2001.* Ah . . . the sweet smell of success.

1968 (139 min.). Keir Dullea, Gary Lockwood, William Sylvester, Daniel Richter. Dir.: Stanley Kubrick.

  VS

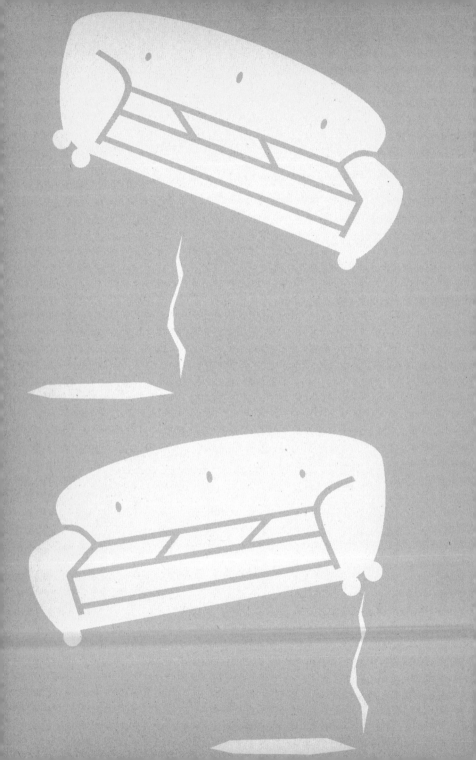

V.
Bad Seeds

Was it Premiere magazine that called the "film" Radioland Murders "a dog with no legs and no tail"? Now, that's bad seed rhetoric at its finest. Bad seed rhetoric, which we've been saving and stewing on for many years; bad seed rhetoric, which foreshadows an area of Baked Potatoes that hints at the—shall we say?—"offensive."

Welcome to the section that isn't afraid to call a piece of shit "a piece of shit." Given limited space and the fact that 99 percent of the movies that come out are complete horse scrotum, we can only review some highlights in the long, incessant history of artistic nonsensibility.

There's nothing better than a movie that sucks so bad you can rag on it till the end of time. Except a whole chapter of them.

Bambi 💣

The life and times of a very special deer.

Should never have been shown to you at the age of seven. The happy ending doesn't bring his mom back, does it? Disney needed to teach the children a little lesson about death, didn't he? DIDN'T HE? A little more than we needed to know at that age, Uncle Waltie. A lot more. And old wounds heal very, very slowly.

A generation scarred with each theatrical rerelease. Now you can finally watch it at home. Oh, joy!

1942 (69 min.). Voices of Stan Alexander, Peter Behn, Cammie King, Bobby Stewart, Fred Shields. Dir.: David Hand.

 VS

Caligula 💣

Why is Uncle Bud dressed up like Caesar?

Caligula is like kissing your old, rasty aunts and uncles on the lips. When you were little it was great. Now it's like being castrated by John Gielgud.

Caligula, Pippi Longstocking, The Dukes of Hazzard . . . remember the unwritten rule (see *Woodstock)* and don't try to reclaim past glories. You were a high school javelin star once. Now you're fat and unaccomplished. You had ambition once. Now you collect cast-iron figurines. For God's sake, please say you don't eat the Filet-o'-Fish. If you or someone you know eats the Filet-o'-Fish, this should be interpreted as a cry for help. Functional individuals do not eat the Filet-o'-Fish.

Let's call a grouper a grouper. *Caligula*'s got potential—bestiality, necrophilia, rape, and dysfunction—but still never quite arrives.

1980 (156 min.). Malcolm McDowell, John Gielgud, Peter O'Toole, Helen Mirren. Dir.: Tinto Brass.

  vs

Carrie 💣

I swear, I didn't talk behind your back.

Some films are truly moving. *Casablanca, Terms of Endearment, Sophie's Choice.* But so is *Carrie.* Halfway through you are moved to a facility where there are people to talk to and you can't hurt yourself anymore. If you're lucky you'll get Dustin Hoffman as a roommate, but chances are you're not. You get Gary Coleman. And he can still talk.

This is one of the most lethal and disturbing bad seeds known to man and a popular late-night TNT/TBS/USA–type entrée. If it comes on the screen, just shut it off. Don't be a hero.

Sissy Spacek, unsettling in the abstract, combines with a movie and the completely unredeeming and terrible tale of teenager taunted by peers. Sure, she gets some revenge with telekinesis, but at what cost? Your health. Unearthing your previous life as an Iditarod sled dog can wait till an official nervous breakdown. Run.

1976 (97 min.). Sissy Spacek, Piper Laurie, John Travolta. Dir.: Brian De Palma.

  vs

The Elephant Man

Dude has giant deformed head.

Bad call.

1980 (125 min.). Anthony Hopkins, John Hurt, Anne Bancroft, John Gielgud, Wendy Hiller, Freddie Jones, Kenny Baker. Dir.: David Lynch.

  vs

Eraserhead

There's this guy whose haircut makes his head look like an eraser, and a chicken baby.

Unwatchable.

1978 (90 min.). John Nance, Charlotte Stewart, Allen Joseph. Dir.: David Lynch.

  D vl

Hudson Hawk 💣

Life-wrecking.

There are not many instances where mass suicide is advisable. Jack in the Box franchisees. Masada. And the *Hudson Hawk* wrap party. The first two happened. The third one should have.

And hence the onslaught began:

VideoHound's Golden Movie Retriever (Visible Ink Press, 1995) calls *Hudson Hawk:* "A big budget star vehicle with little else going for it. Everyone in the cast tries to be extra funny, resulting in a disjointed situation where no one is. Weakly plotted, poorly paced." (Rating: one dog bone.)

Movies on TV and Videocassette calls *Hudson Hawk:* "For the birds—one of the worst films in recent years. Caper 'comedy' about a cat burglar coaxed out of retirement to steal da Vinci originals. It is as bad as its reputation."

Random passerby on the street calls *Hudson Hawk:* "Cat food. I'd rather eat my foot."

The movie that galvanized the sympathy of an entire nation.

Agony.

1991 (95 min.). Bruce Willis, Danny Aiello, Andie MacDowell, James Coburn, Sandra Bernhard, Richard E. Grant, Frank Stallone. Dir.: Michael Lehmann.

     VS

Ishtar 💣

Untalented singers travel to Middle East, become involved in high-stakes web of international un-intrigue.

It's not every skak film that makes it into the hallowed confines of the Jersey Shwag Hall of Fame. If it were, the building would consume more square footage than the ever-expanding Gene Siskel. For Christ's sake, it'd be one giant parlor of Michael Dudikoffs and Patrick Swayzes. Although that's something people would definitely get baked and pay to see. Hmmmm. Sounds like one for BP Development:

> Michael Dudikoff and Patrick Swayze in the self-effacing black comedy of two men imprisoned in Gene Siskel's stomach fighting over who is the less talented actor and should therefore eat the other to survive. Kind of a story of being eaten inside a story of being eaten. Kind of *Jonah and the Whale* meets *Alive* meets *My Dinner with Andre*. Ethan Hawke directs. Shot on location. Call it: *Eating Dudi.*

Back in the Hall of Fame, kudos to Dustin Hoffman and Warren Beatty, who aren't afraid to play two scathingly bad musicians gigging in some Middle Eastern hellhole. Of course, they get mixed up in espionage and escape capture in a very Gumpian way.

Ishtar takes it's rightful place on the wall of legends: *Hudson Hawk, Nosferatu the Vampyre, Highlander II.* Shwag historians must attend.

1987 (107 min.). Dustin Hoffman, Warren Beatty, Isabelle Adjani, Charles Grodin. Dir.: Elaine May.

  VS

Jurassic Park 💣

It's amazing what they can do with computers these days.

Sans the C.G. dinosaurs, *Jurassic Park* was many things: a humiliating display of bad acting (special notice going to Richard Attenborough); a seminar on how not to adapt a bestselling novel; and either a parody or a pale imitation of Steven Spielberg's filmmaking. And all shot on a Universal Studio's theme-park ride. And maybe it was more than that . . .

Call it pot-induced paranoia, but it feels like the only part that ol' Steve actually had his hand in was the T-rex attack, not coincidentally the single good moment in the movie, and the only one you ever see "behind the scenes" footage of him actually on the set. Hard to direct a good dinosaur flick when you're in Poland making *Schindler's List,* eh Steve? Just let the gnomes in the basement of the Skywalker Ranch clean things up on their computer terminals, and everything'll be hunky-dory. Lend your good name to the project and you, Mike Crichton, and the suits at Universal can laugh to the tune of a billion dollars worldwide.

A totally baked conspiracy theory? Could be. But regardless of who was at the wheel, one thing is certain: Shrunk to the small screen, *Jurassic Park* is exposed for what it truly is—a low-budget schlock-fest with a zillion dollars worth of amazing special effects. It should be left at the bottom of the bag, with the rest of the shake.

1993 (126 min.). Sam Neill, Laura Dern, Jeff Goldblum, Richard Attenborough, Samuel L. Jackson. Dir.: Steven Spielberg?

        VS

Meet the Feebles 💣

Did you ever wonder what went on backstage at The Muppet Show?

Other questions to ponder while watching *The Feebles,* right before someone's finally had the common sense to say "Will somebody please stop this fiasco!":

Is everybody OK? Did we really just see a giant walrus puppet screwing a little cat puppet? What sick mind actually came up with the idea to show characters based on the Muppets masturbate, shoot up heroin, piss and shit themselves in mass quantities, contract VD, make underground porno flicks, and blow each other away with machine guns? What freak show recommended this winner? Was there an Old Shmoo, and if so, was it those blob guys from *The Herculoids?* Who took the time to actually choreograph those countless and interminable musical numbers? Who took the time to make this movie? Why did the Baked Potatoes staff actually watch this film a second time, after the first viewing was rejected at the ten-minute mark? And why did the book even bother to include this hard-to-find cult film in any way, shape, or form, which could be interpreted as a vindictive attempt to bamboozle the readers into renting the damn thing so they can feel just as unpleasant and emotionally soiled as the authors do?

Rent it. We dare you. We double-dare you.

1989 (100 min.). Dir.: Peter Jackson.

The Money Tree 💣

Preachy, cannabiographical, nuclear holocaust of donkey ass.

The Money Tree needs to be addressed. Certainly not on its merits as a good story, told well. Certainly not for its acting. Certainly not for much.

It needs to be addressed as it highlights a pitfall to which we are all subject. *The Money Tree* is a self-flagellating, transparent debacle illustrating what happens when a heavy pot smoker gets stuck in the delusion that he has the greatest idea ever created. Normally, you wake up the next day and realize that an entire film about a Frisbee or dollar-grilled-cheese just doesn't cut it for ninety minutes. Couple not waking up with grandpa's cash and you've got your very own *Money Tree;* something like a Chia Pet but far worse.

In this case, the greatest idea ever created is a movie about a drug dealer battling society to harvest his crop complete with subtext implying filmmakers did same to finance the project. The film got a lot of press, and in a vacuum the idea really isn't that bad. It's just that outside that vacuum, in your VCR, it sucks.

The whole way through, everyone at BP Central was rooting for these guys. Please let this be stoners make good. Please let this get better. Please tell us this isn't happening. Now, we're embarrassed.

In all fairness, there is one brilliantly stoned moment hidden in *The Money Tree*. It's almost worth the cost of rental. Hint: sax.

1992 (94 min.). Christopher Dienstag. Dir.: Alan Dienstag.

   𝓗

Naked Lunch

Overwrought, self-indulgent, angst-ridden moose shit.

BP Intelligence tells us that specifically, "Naked Lunch" is a moment conceived of by William S. Burroughs. A moment in a restaurant, at lunch, when everything is suddenly frozen, revealing the morsels of food, stuck in midstroke, distilled for an instant and visible on the forks of all patrons. In addition to the moment, *Naked Lunch,* the movie, examines the strange and symbolic world of heroin-addicted exterminators.

Now, that's Baked Potato material. Unfortunately the transition from book to screen was a bit like *An American Werewolf in London.* Good-looking kid turns into beast. This baby is the definition of a bad seed. A Cronenberg film you think would be perfect high but ends up with no story, twisted but pointless looks, lots of roaches you can't smoke, and general headache-inducing artistic masturbation. *Naked Lunch* should come with a free side of Advil.

1991 (115 min.). Peter Weller, Judy Davis, Ian Holm, Roy Scheider. Dir.: David Cronenberg.

☠   𝓥𝓢

Nosferatu the Vampyre 💣

The German remake of the very first vampire flick comes with its sympathies clearly in the count's corner.

The baddest seed of 'em all. The worst film to watch stoned ever made. Bar none. Chairman Pryde was overheard to say, "Any movie that makes *El Topo* look this fuckin' good is a disaster of epic proportions!" Well-spoken.

There are three scenes in this film. Bruno Ganz is walking somewhere, and looking for someone or something. A carriage is traveling down a country lane. And every now and then, they cut to pasty-faced Klaus Kinski sneering with what appears to be a two-pronged plastic fork between his teeth. That's it.

These moments are repeated ad infinitum, all to the dulcet tones of theme music that eases you quietly into the reassuring embrace of a coma. The characters don't speak. They contemplate. They stare into nothingness. For minutes at a time. Oh, the joy of watching a big-name European artiste like Werner Herzog reinvent the vampire myth. He captures the true essence of real-time horse travel in the nineteenth century. Viewers actually experience the hours of tedium as if they were truly there.

Hey Werner, here's a little friendly advice: Krazy Klaus lapping at Isabelle Adjani's beautiful neck doesn't butter the biscuit. Next time you make a vampire flick . . . *give us some fucking blood sucking!!!!!!!*

1979 (107 min.). Klaus Kinski, Isabelle Adjani, Bruno Ganz. Dir.: Werner Herzog.

Nosferatu the Vampyre

So bad it warrants another review.

Top ten things you would gladly be subjected to rather than watching a movie where nothing happens except endless and mind-piercing travel sequences in a carriage (i.e., *Nosferatu the Vampyre*):

10) Full-body coating with I Can't Believe It's Not Butter spray.
9) Your grandparents naked with sexual toys and aids.
8) The warden from *Story of Ricky*.
7) A top-ten list.
6) Televised bowling.
5) Incurable and lifelong constipation not treatable with shredded wheat and forcing you to shit out of some bizarre and uncomely plastic tubing.
4) *El Topo*.
3) Rabies.
2) Zima.

And the number one thing you would gladly be subjected to rather than watching the ultimate bad seed, *Nosferatu the Vampyre:*

1) Howie Mandel.

Believe it.

1979 (107 min.). Klaus Kinski, Isabelle Adjani, Bruno Ganz. Dir.: Werner Herzog.

The Rocky Horror Picture Show 💣

You can sit down now.

Sorry, people who throw rice, transvestites, and Meatloaf. It's just that this film's the biggest ruse since precooked weights.

Let's look past the fact that *Rocky Horror*=self-deception. We're similar after all. You dress up for movies, we get fried. Both rituals have an unfair stigma attached to them. Both are considered "abnormal." Both are subcultures far more capable than our present government.

What would happen if Baked Potatoes took over the world? Guess it would be a little like *Invasion of the Body Snatchers* except with potato-looking things instead of pea pods. Boy, would that change everything.

Balanced budget? Who cares. Defense spending? Sure, we like *Star Wars.* Welfare? Better than work. Infrastructure? If everyone would just drive at the same rate there'd be no traffic.

And . . . as a show of good faith, we stock the Supreme Court with *Rocky Horror* freaks.

Fair?

1975 (95 min.). Tim Curry, Susan Sarandon, Barry Bostwick, Meatloaf, Little Nell, Richard O'Brien. Dir.: Jim Sharman.

    VS

Target Tornado 💣

". . . A compelling quest for tornados . . ."

In our vast and widespread search for the ultimate in quality and unsung baked pleasure, it was only a matter of time before we turned to one of cable's most reliable high-pressure systems . . . the Weather Channel.

We're not afraid to come out of the basement and admit it: We watch the Weather Channel. A lot. "The Five-Day Business Planner," "The Traveler's Forecast," "Your Local Forecast" . . . not to mention the titillating graphs and charismatic meteorological personalities.

It was but a natural extension of our faith in the network that when *Target Tornado* was advertized as a Weather Channel "Home Video Collection Special Presentation," we expected an El Niño of gale-force proportion. We expected forty minutes of heart-pounding thunderstorming opera, charging the emotional cyclone toward real-life tornado death and carnage. We expected trailer homes ripped from the ground, sucked two hundred feet in the air, torn to shreds, and blasted apart; fast-food establishments, McDonald's Playlands, leveled and snapped in two tokes; hospitals and elementary schools turned to atomic dust before our very eyes. We wanted havoc. And we wanted it bad.

What we got was sleet. No carnage. No death. No anarchy. No justice. Not even a delayed opening. Just Dr. I'madorkweatherman, the history of tornadoes and how they are formed, and a bunch of losers in little tornado-mobiles chasing funnel clouds.

About fifteen minutes in, the travesty becomes apparent. Of course, there's no carnage. If you're that close to the thing, you're dead. Incidentally, that's the only quality moment in the film—a clip in which the tornado approaches and eventually kills the cameraman. But even this is anticlimactic, as the device cuts to black immediately rather than getting launched into the sky while still recording. Damn.

We anted up the $19.95 plus $3.95 shipping and handling, and we're here to tell you: *don't*. The "free" thermometer–key chain is the only thing worth looking at.

1995 (45 min.). 1-800-519-8885 to order this and other Weather Channel products.

The Terror of Tiny Town 💣

Western, with demented but rather effective hook.

"Quaint . . . Performed by the first all-midget musical cast ever to make a feature . . . The hard-riding, two-gun boys go buckety-buck on Shetland ponies. The heroine escapes the villain by running under the furniture instead of around it . . ."—*Hollywood Reporter*

"Cowboys walk under saloon doors, chase beneath barroom tables, and ride off into the sunset on Shetland ponies . . ."—*Cayman Island Times*

"Miniature romance."—*Variety*

How can you go wrong with a solid buzz and an all-midget Western?
It's possible.
High on concept, short on talent.
And who gives a shit about Shetland ponies?

1938 (63 min.). Billy Curtis, Yvonne Moray. Dir.: Sam Newfield.

        VL

Toys 💣

Unintelligible, misguided, cybershwag meets FAO Schwartz cross-blended clusterfuck.

We wouldn't waste the space if it wasn't urgent. In case you were out of sorts, in case you saw Barry Levinson, Robin Williams, and *Toys* on the box and thought "good choice," in case you forgot your medication . . .
DON'T RENT *TOYS*.
Fifty million dollars and Barry Levinson comes home with this? Rather have a barrel of lizard shit. Fifty million dollars and we get a story about a toy factory set in *Brave New World?* What we could have done with fifty mil. Bought a bag. Started a fund to help Robert Townsend get back on track.

Sorry, Barry, we loved *Diner* and you gave Steve Guttenberg a fighting chance and you seem like an OK guy, but what happened here? Willy Wonka and Aldous Huxley got trapped in that fly machine with Jeff Goldblum? Tell us it was excessive drug use; we'll understand. Tell us you were captured by aliens who traded your brain for that of a moth larva; we'll understand. Tell us LL Cool J pistol-whipped you; we'll understand.

Please, Barry, tell us something. Anything.

1992 (121 min.). Robin Williams, Joan Cusack, Michael Gambon, LL Cool J, Robin Wright. Dir.: Barry Levinson.

Watership Down

Evicted rabbits in search of housing upgrade.

A true story: Four people are in a car, it's a sunny fall day with leaves all around. They're all tripping and should absolutely not be on the road. No one's saying anything, just the sounds of grinding teeth and various trinkets being mauled into confetti by rubbing hands. Finally, the guy driving turns to the girl sitting shotgun and says, "I am tripping my head off." She says, "Yeah, me too." He says, "Thank God I'm not driving."

Now, the makers of *Watership Down* were clearly not in the car, because if they were they wouldn't have created a guaranteed bug-out animated nightmare about rabbits. There was a time when people had a dog, a cat, one smart kid, one stupid kid, no sex life, and they were happy. Now everyone needs a New Age pet. Ferrets, monkeys, iguanas, fladermice, baby pigs for Christ's sake. Maybe it's a nod to law enforcement, but doubtful. And rabbits. The only nice thing about rabbits is ear muffs.

Wear a hat and skip it.

1978 (92 min.). Voices of Ralph Richardson, Zero Mostel, John Hurt. Dir.: Martin Rosen.

Epilogue

Baked Potatoes are smart. They're sensitive. They're dirty and deformed. But it doesn't mean they're perfect. In our quest to review a limited number of the most relevant pot-smoking videos of all time, there is a remote possibility we overlooked a few classics, a tiny cadre of unsung heroes, some resistant bad seeds . . . your personal favorite baked movie of all time. Spare us the "you know nothing about pot or movies" crap. When was the last time you spent a year getting baked and watching films for a living? The last nine years? Fine, you have a drug problem. Congratulations.

Anyway, there's no time to hate. Just send in your suggestions or reviews to P.O. Box 2208, Wilmington, N.C. 28402, or reach us at the BP Web site at http://www.sonicnet.com/baked, and the BPAC will consider them, in closed session, for inclusion in the upcoming runaway bestseller: *Baked Potatoes II: (More Baked) Potatoes*. There's still considerable support for *Baked Potatoes II: I Play Tetris and Am Obese*, but that's our problem, not yours.

Lastly, it goes without saying that *Baked Potatoes* and its proud publisher, Doubleday, clearly do not advocate the use of illicit drugs. Nor do we support prescription drugs. Let the infection run its course.

Appendix I
Distributors

The tools of our trade are not always at arm's reach. The quest is half the fun, however, and the rewards of a hard-fought search are often manifold. Should your local video store be unable to provide you with the necessary materials, or if you'd simply prefer to not move from your place of comfort, listed below are a select handful of connoisseurs whose business it is to help:

ⅅ Dave's Videodrome

The quintessential B.P. video den. By potatoes, for potatoes.

405 East Main Street, Carrboro, NC 27510
Phone: 919-968-8482
Fax: 919-968-8562
E-mail: djimenez@nando.net
Dave's Bio:

Dave's Videodrome is housed in a low-profile storefront in Carrboro, North Carolina, in the building that was once the Hollywood Theater, which specialized in blaxploitation and kung fu flicks during the 1970s. Dave Jimenez, the proprietor, has spent the last twenty-odd years searching out weird and obscure films and videos in a futile attempt to satisfy his insatiable movie jones. After exhausting the resources of all local rental outlets, he decided that the only way he would get to see gems like *Nekromantik* and *Story of Ricky* would be to open his own video store. The rest is history.

In addition to the best of Hollywood and independent cinema, Dave has the largest selection of Hong Kong films and Japanese animation in North Carolina. Services include rental by mail, free searches for rare and out-of-print videotapes and laser discs, and preorder discounts on tapes and discs. As this book goes to press, Dave is preparing the first issue of a new magazine, *Movie Freak*.

Walk-in membership is free with photo i.d. Visa or MasterCard required for rental by mail. Write, call, fax, or E-mail for details.

P.S. Beware Dave's personal recommendations.

F Facet's Video

Big, busy, but vast selection.

Phone: 1-800-532-2387 and you need a membership
Rental and purchase

Basic Rent-by-Mail Membership: twenty-five dollars, which includes two free rentals. Film Critic Membership: one hundred dollars, which includes twelve free rentals. Catalogs also available . . . for a price.

Visa/MasterCard, AmEx, Discover required.

VL Video Library

Reasonable, rational, professional, cool.

7157 Germantown Avenue, Philadelphia, PA 19119-1842
Phone: 800-669-7157
Fax: 215-248-5627
Rentals only, VHS, 10–9 EST, 7 days

Nationwide rental rate: six dollars per title plus round-trip shipping for three nights (honor system). No membership fee. Outgoing via UPS or Priority Mail; reusable shipper comes with correct postage for mailbox returns.

Reservations taken for absent titles. Strong cult, foreign, Baked Potato, and vintage holdings. Advance order of ten titles brings discounted shipping at regular intervals. *Video Stores:* no. *Catalog:* free. *Shipping:* varies per order zone. Visa/MasterCard, AmEx, Discover; check/money order; no COD.

Appendix II
Troubleshooting:
Coping with a Bad Seed

On some occasions nature's bounty turns on you. Paranoia? A powerful hunch the world will end within the next four minutes? Taken aback by an unexpected Patrick Swayze cameo? *Don't fight it!* Refer below for step-by-step resuscitation procedures.

One Alarm

1. Enter bathroom, wash your face, take a drink of water. *Do not* look in the mirror for more than three minutes.
2. Return to living room and say out loud: "Wow, this is really good pot." See if anyone agrees. If no response, refer to "Three Alarms."

Two Alarms

1. Stop tape, pray for rerun of: *The Love Boat, Fantasy Island, Magnum, P.I.,* or any Stephen J. Cannell production.
2. Have another bong hit.

Three Alarms

1. Say out loud: "You think this pot was laced?" See if anyone agrees. If no response, refer to "Four Alarms."
2. Don't start monitoring your heart rate.

Four Alarms

1. *Do not* call your parents.
2. Curl up in fetal position and insist on being taken to hospital.

Appendix III
The Gold Circle

In our ongoing effort to seek harmony with the outside world, the BPAC recommended we create an "Acapulco Gold Circle" of outstanding businesses, products, and individual honorees. Presented herein are samples of the generous and affectionate spirit in which we reached out to our deserving brothers and sisters. None of whom responded.

Jeannie Duisenberg
Public Relations, Lockheed
P.O. Box 3504, Organization 24-01, Building 101
Sunnyvale, CA 94088-3504

Dear Jeannie:

We know it seems strange that we would write to you about the upcoming felony flambé <u>Baked Potatoes: A Pot Smoker's Guide to Film and Video</u>, but the fact is that pot smokers love technology, especially weapons. We've been painted by the media as these tree-hugging, dolphin-humping commies but we, at least some of us, can appreciate a quality F-14 Tomcat or that high-pitch whiz of a Scud missile.

Anyway, what we're trying to say is even though we come at it from different directions we both have a passion for power and precision. For you it's a business. For us it's entertainment. Maybe that's why they call it the entertainment business. Anyway, the point is that our BP Advisory Committee has recommended you as a fine defense-systems entity. A "groovy" weapons maker as the kids these days might phrase it. We'd like to include you in our Acapulco Gold section as Best Weapons Maker.

We hope this is OK. If we don't hear back in two weeks (our deadline), we'll assume it's OK to include you in the text. In addition, the committee has asked us to contact you in the hopes of receiving your spring catalog. Do you have a consumer publication, like an L.L. Bean or Victoria's Secret thing where we could call up and order weaponry via an 800 number?

Sincerely:

<u>Baked Potatoes</u> Authors
Michael Wexler
John Hulme

cc: R. Parish, H. N. Schwarzkopf

Hunt/Wesson
C/O Phillip Mangiracina (Orville Redenbacher's Popcorn)
1645 Valencia Drive
Fullerton, CA 92633

Dear Phillip:

We're writing to you in reference to the upcoming kernel of kind <u>Baked Potatoes: A Pot Smoker's Guide to Film and Video</u>. While it won't solve the eternal question of why some corns never pop, it does rate films as to their relative agony or ecstasy during a cannabis-influenced viewing.

As we both know, popcorn is intricately connected to film, and marijuana is intricately connected to eating, hence popcorn is related to pot and hence to you.

After a gallant and exhaustive research, our BP Advisory Committee has picked your popcorn as the nominee for our Acapulco Gold Circle's Best Popcorn, to be included in the text. Paul Newman put up a good fight, but not good enough.

We know it sounds ridiculous, but <u>Baked Potatoes</u> is quite real. Other nominees for the Gold Circle include Blockbuster, Butterfinger, and others. Hundreds of thousands of pot-smoking Americans will read this book and focus their patronage toward those companies willing to show their support for <u>Baked Potatoes</u> by accepting a place in the Gold Circle. If we don't hear back from you in writing within two weeks (our deadline) we'll assume it's OK with your department to list the popcorn. Congratulations, again!

Sincerely:

<u>Baked Potatoes</u> Authors
Michael Wexler
John Hulme

May Orville rest in peace.

Todd Thompson
Butterfinger Marketing
800 North Brand Boulevard
Glendale, CA 91203

Dear Todd:

There's something about a Butterfinger that makes you want to claw your eyes out. We think it's when you're really stoned and it's stuck in all your teeth and suddenly you start having a terrible flashback about Jack and the Beanstalk clubbing Alice in Wonderland to death.

You see, that's the kind of unbridled humor featured in the upcoming pita pocket with the mostest <u>Baked Potatoes: A Pot Smoker's Guide to Film and Video</u>. In all seriousness, though, our BP Advisory Committee, composed of top men and women helping us with the text, have elected Butterfinger to our highly elite Acapulco Gold Circle as the Best Candy Bar for Really Stoned People. We know it sounds ridiculous, but we assure you, <u>Baked Potatoes</u> is quite legitimate. Other nominees include Blockbuster, Orville Redenbacher, and Depend Undergarments.

Some companies feel a slight touchiness about the pot issue, even though most people in the companies are addicted to alcohol, caffeine, or cocaine themselves, but gauging from Butterfinger's psychedelic advertising campaign we figured you guys would be cool. Pot smokers love candy, and our endorsement may really swing a large demographic in your direction.

If we don't hear back from you in writing within two weeks (our deadline) we'll assume it's gonna be OK with your corp. relations people to list you in this section as one of our principal supporters and recommended products.

Sincerely

<u>Baked Potatoes</u> Authors
Michael Wexler
John Hulme

Blockbuster Corporation
1 Blockbuster Plaza
Ft. Lauderdale, FL 33301
Attn.: Ted Innes

Dear Ted:

We're writing to you with regards to the upcoming crown jewel <u>Baked Potatoes: A Pot Smoker's Guide to Film and Video</u>, due out next season from Doubleday. Perhaps you've already heard about it?

Regardless, the text reviews films as to their efficacy during a marijuana-influenced viewing. Although none of us is pleased about the horrible scourge that drugs have wrought upon our society, we must face the fact that pot and film are intimately related. It's almost as American as baseball and apple pie—except illegal. People take drugs, though, drugs don't take drugs, so let's not blame the messenger.

Anyway, the reason we're contacting you is to congratulate you on being elected to our Acapulco Gold Circle of Ultimate Video Stores for Really Stoned People. In addition, we'd like to see how many in-store copies you might require for your various franchises.

We're sure you're aware of the long history of video and alternative culture and the growing scope and financial power of this demographic. As one of the leaders in crystallizing this cannabinoid movement, we invite you into our circle of honorees. If we don't hear from you in writing within two weeks (our deadline) we'll assume it's OK to recommend Blockbuster to the thousands of fried customers awaiting our Gold Circle picks.

Sincerely:

<u>Baked Potatoes</u> Authors
Michael Wexler
John Hulme

From: Roger Ebert
To: John Hulme
Date: Mon, Jan 9, 1995, 7:14 PM
RE: Video Reviews

Sorry, but I don't have any interest in your book, which strikes me as being rather wrongheaded, since presumably any movie is more or less the same if you're stoned. Why would one want to cloud one's sensibilities in order to see a movie?
Best,
RE

Distribution:
   John Hulme

Appendix IV
The Food Quotient

For decades, film and food have gone hand in hand. Reliable evidence also points to an intimate relationship between cannabis and appetite. Hence, The Food Quotient, a simple but essential scale for evaluating your dining options during the viewing experience.

Food:	(((Quality+	Affordability*	+ Ease)
McDonald's	7	7	5
McDonald's breakfast	9.5	7	3
Pizza delivered	8	5	9
Pizza picked up	9	7	4
Pizza bought with Competitor's Coupons (In Appendix IX)	9.5	10	4
Ben & Jerry's	7	5	6
"The White Rose System," 154 Woodbridge Ave., Highland Park, NJ	10	10	10
Chips and salsa	7	7	4
Wings	8	5	3
Grilled cheese	7	9	3
Popcorn	5	9	6
Another bong hit	10	9	10
Nothing	0	10	1
Your cat	1	10	10
Long John Silver's	0	0	0

*(Quantity + Price)÷2

- Gastronomical Debit)	x π)	= TFQ
3	π	16π
5	π	14.5π
4	π	18π
4	π	16π
4	π	19.5π
0	π	18π
10	π	20π
5	π	13π
4	π	12π
1	π	18π
2	π	18π
0	π	29π
5	π	6π
10	π	11π
10	π	−10π

Appendix V
Red-Haired Moments

The following are little moments of sheer brilliance tucked neatly inside films that failed to meet the rigid criteria of inclusion in *Baked Potatoes*. They may or may not be worth renting in their entirety, but if you're fortunate to stumble onto an entry in your local Sunday TV supplement, settle down, light up, and relish these tasty little slices of genius pie.

Scene Work

The car chase in *Bullitt*.
The car chase in *The French Connection*.
Chuck Norris cracking a beer and driving his pickup right out of the ground in *Lone Wolf McQuade*.
The final battle in *Glory*.
Any action sequence in *Menace II Society*.
Any scene between Richard Dreyfuss and the ticket guy in *Let It Ride*.
Twin Peaks: Fire Walk with Me: David Bowie and the closed-circuit monitors.
"I could've been a contender."
William Hickey offering Anjelica Huston a cookie in *Prizzi's Honor*.
The opening tracking shot in *Touch of Evil*.
Any action sequence in *La Femme Nikita* (especially the opening).
Christopher Walken vs. Dennis Hopper in *True Romance*.
The chase scene on the Chicago el and up the parking ramp in *The Hunter*.

Dr. Lecter escaping in *The Silence of the Lambs*.

The Zen loogie in *Revenge of the Nerds II*.

The graduation scene in *Fame*.

The apartment conversation in *Breathless* (Godard).

The vessel with the pestle and the flagon with the dragon in *The Court Jester*.

Jack Nicholson ordering some toast in *Five Easy Pieces*.

The end of *The Passenger*.

The *Potemkin*-like scene in *The Untouchables*.

The buffalo hunt in *Dances with Wolves*.

The heist in *Rififi*.

The heist in *Topkapi*.

The supermarket robbery sequence in *Raising Arizona*.

Dan Hedaya being buried alive in *Blood Simple*.

The hotel burning up in *Barton Fink*.

The deathbed composing between Tom Hulce and F. Murray Abraham in *Amadeus*.

Darkman's killer handshake.

The unbelievable patience of *North by Northwest*'s crop-duster sequence.

The school-yard sequence in *The Birds*—get those little brats . . .

Notorious.

Dinner conversation between Alec Baldwin, Fred Ward, and Jennifer Jason Leigh in *Miami Blues*.

Toecutter meeting his maker in *Mad Max*.

The devil stealing souls in *Highway 61*.

The opening tracking shot in *The Player*—the three principals are still alive.

Any speech and the final battle in *Henry V*.

The entrance of Orson Welles and the tunnel sequences in *The Third Man*.

The chariot race in *Ben-Hur*.

The paranoia of Ray Liotta's arrest in *GoodFellas*.

The drill sergeant's opening tirade in *Full Metal Jacket*.

The museum romance in *Dressed to Kill*.

Rodney Dangerfield's happy home in *Natural Born Killers*.

The sharing of a romance novel between Anthony Hopkins and Emma Thompson in *The Remains of the Day*.

The final stunt in *Hooper*.

Re-runs of *Hooperman*.

The first Russian roulette sequence in *The Deer Hunter*.

The poolroom fight sequence in *Mean Streets*.

Steve McQueen, head through the jail-cell door, not turning on Dustin Hoffman in *Papillon*.

The "double gobble/there he is" scene in *Vernon, Florida*.

The Jimi Hendrix Vietnam soldier/Cleopatra monologue-riff and Hawaiian guitar jam in *Rainbow Bridge*.

This Sporting Life

The football game in *The Longest Yard*.

The pregame warm-up in *North Dallas Forty*.

The football game in *M*A*S*H*.

The final game in *The Natural*.

The final game in *Hoosiers*.

The soccer game in *Victory*.

Bruce Lee vs. Chuck Norris in *Return of the Dragon*.

Actually, any Bruce Lee'll do.

The bike race in *Breaking Away*.

Jackie Chan's final fight in *The Big Brawl*.

The guitar duel from *Crossroads* (1986) . . . Ralph Macchio: the high priest of guitar.

Mel Gibson's futile sprint in *Gallipoli*. Actually, that's a pretty depressing scene.

The final wrestling match in *Paradise Alley*.

Snake Plissken vs. Ox Baker in *Escape from New York*.

Any race in *Chariots of Fire*.

Ladies and gentlemen, boys and girls . . . dyin' time's here—*Mad Max Beyond Thunderdome*.

Minnesota Fats and Fast Eddie Felson play a little pool in *The Hustler*.

Vincent and "The Werewolves of London" in *The Color of Money*.

The boxing sequences in *Raging Bull*.

The climactic fight in *Bad Boys*.

Short Cuts

The first ten minutes of *Freaked*.
The final act of *Trilogy of Terror*.
The final ten minutes of *Rear Window*.
The final ten minutes of *Witness*.
"The Crate" episode from *Creepshow*.
The last twenty minutes of *Do the Right Thing*.
The opening ten minutes of *Zentropa*.
The first twenty minutes of *Wild at Heart*.
The climax of *Scarface* (De Palma).
Any thirty minutes of *Nashville*.

Death and Mayhem

Any kill in *Friday the 13th,* parts 1–4, 7.
Any gore-splattered scene in *Dead Alive*.
The killing of the hiking family in *Prophecy*.
The nurse getting toasted in *The Exorcist 3*.
The first three kills in *The Fog*.
The guy trapped under the ice in *Damien—Omen II*.
Martin Balsam getting the raddish in *Psycho*.
The guy under the elevator in *The Fly II*.
The guy from *Fame* getting squeezed through the door in the 1988
    remake of *The Blob*.
The guy with the hammer getting skewered in *Conan the Barbarian*.

Concepts to Savor as You Watch

The utter excess of the making of *Cleopatra*.
How somebody thought the imbecilic plotline of *Highlander II: The
    Quickening* might actually work.
The fantasy that *The Lord of the Rings* will be correctly animated one
    day in the future.
The kids' room (and Swiss army knife) in *The Double McGuffin*.

The hatred you feel for the British after watching *Breaker Morant* and
In the Name of the Father.

The level of futility reached by *Radioland Murders,* the dog with no
legs or tail. And the fact that the authors of this book are in the
band, and visibly baked onscreen, for most of the film.

Appendix VI
Planet of the Apes

... the real reason to lose your mind over this fine series of films is the desperate situation that the aforementioned former child star of *My Friend Flicka*'s career seems to be in considering the fact that the tightly cyclical continuity of the Apes movies doesn't seem to allow for another entry and there seems little support for a new TV series since the last one starring two journeymen character actors who looked unfortunately like Starsky and Hutch was given the justifiable hook by the network suits who knew full well that America wasn't ready to accept the admittedly bizarre yet charmingly affected manner of our man Roddy Mac on a weekly basis but only on a one-week-a-year basis, the second most eagerly anticipated 4:30 Movie special of the year, known as "Apes Week," which was popular enough to generate the cotton industry of Apes merchandise such as the Apes Tree House and the Forbidden Zone and the Dr. Zeus doll, which brings to mind the uncomfortable memory of that moment when you stretched the Cornelius and Urko dolls into an unnatural position and their interior rubber bands snapped and the arms and legs fell out of their sockets and all you were left with was a plastic head and a torso and isn't that a pleasant thing to think about just when your high has kicked in and your own personal rubber band is snapping and leaving behind nothing but a useless hunk of flesh that was once a human being and let's talk about something more positive shall we such as the location of the one and only Baked Potatoes Treasure Chest which is buried somewhere amidst the highways and byways of this once great nation beneath the same soft earth from which all life on this planet returns to at one time or another and there is a pirate's trove of wonders contained within this box in the ground and the only way to find out where is to send away for the Baked Potatoes Treasure Map which can be ordered by mailing an SASE with your address on it to Baked Potatoes Treasure Map c/o *Baked Potatoes* P.O. Box 2208 Wilmington NC 28402 and we promise you will not be disappointed when you unearth this glorious prize if you are lucky enough to find it and find it first and it will feel much like the first time you saw the Statue of Liberty scene in the first *Planet of the Apes* when it all came together and Charlie "I once played major biblical figures in major biblical epics but now shill light beers over the radio" Heston fell to his knees in the cold wet sand and you fell with him and it brings back so many chills even talking about it that you need to turn to the sidebar of the *Element of Crime* review so we can continue to muse about the *Planet of the Apes* in one incredible exercise in random self-indulgence . . .

Appendix VII
Supplementary Reading

Abel, Ernest. *A Comprehensive Guide to the Cannabis Literature*. Westport, Conn.: Greenwood Press, 1979.

———. *Marihuana: The First Twelve Thousand Years*. New York: Plenum Press, 1980.

———. *A Marihuana Dictionary: Words, Terms, Events, and Persons Relating to Cannabis*. Westport, Conn.: Greenwood Press, 1982.

———. *I'm So Stoned, Somebody Please Stop Me from Writing Pot Books*. Westport, Conn.: Lost Children Teepee, 1996.

Adler, Patricia A. *Wheeling and Dealing: An Ethnography of an Upper-Level Drug-Dealing and Smuggling Community*. New York: Columbia University Press, 1985.

Anderson, James William. *How to Live Rent Free: Also Mortgage Free, Tax Free (Legally), Job Free (Soon), and Energy Free*. New York: Brun Press, 1980.

Asimov, Isaac, ed. *Baker's Dozen: Thirteen Short Fantasy Novels*. New York: Greenwich House, 1984.

Bates, Marston. *A Jungle in the House: Essays in Natural and Unnatural History*. New York: Walker, 1970.

Bradbury, Malcolm. *Eating People Is Wrong*. Chicago: Academy Chicago Publishers, 1986.

Chapple, Steve. *Outlaws in Babylon: Shocking True Adventures on the Marijuana Frontier*. New York: Pocket Books, 1984.

Conners, Martin, and Julia Furtaw, eds. *VideoHound's Golden Movie Retriever*. Detroit: Visible Ink Press, 1995.

Curtis, Patricia. *Dogs on the Case: Search Dogs Who Help Save Lives and Enforce the Law*. (Photographed by David Cupp.) New York: Lodestar Books, 1989.

Demers, David P. *Breaking Your Child's TV Addiction*. Minneapolis: Marquette Books, 1989.

Denby, David, ed. *Awake in the Dark: An Anthology of American Film Criticism, 1915 to the Present*. New York: Vintage Books, 1977.

Division of Lung Diseases. *Do I Have a Chronic Cough?* Bethesda: U.S. Department of Health and Human Services, 1989.

Donkin, Scott W. *Sitting on the Job: How to Survive the Stresses of Sitting Down to Work: A Practical Handbook*. Boston: Houghton Mifflin, 1989.

Dwyer, Peter D. *The Pigs That Ate the Garden: A Human Ecology from Papua New Guinea*. Ann Arbor: University of Michigan Press, 1990.

Edelman, Peter G., ed. *Biosensors and Chemical Sensors: Optimizing Performance Through Polymeric Materials*. Washington: American Chemical Society, 1992.

F. R. Kets de Vries Manfred and Associates. *Organizations on the Couch: Clinical Perspectives on Organizational Behavior and Change*. San Francisco: Jossey-Bass, 1991.

Gallagher, Patrick G. *The Management and Disposition of Seized Assets*. Washington: U.S. Department of Justice, 1992.

Gilbert, Henry. *Hydroponics: Nutrient Film Techniques*. Beltsville, Md.: National Agriculture Library, 1992.

Glasser, William. *Positive Addiction*. New York: Harper & Row, 1976.

Goldstein, Jay A. *Chronic Fatigue Syndrome: The Limbic Hypothesis*. New York: Haworth Medical Press, 1993.

Greene, Carla. *I Want to Be a Baker*. Chicago: Children's Press, 1956.

Hall, Lindsey, and Leigh Cohn, eds. *Recoveries: True Stories by People Who Conquered Addictions and Compulsions*. Carlsbad, Calif.: Gurze Books, 1987.

Hicks, Robert D. *In Pursuit of Satan: The Police and the Occult*. Buffalo: Prometheus Books, 1991.

Hudnell, Kenneth. *Exposure of Humans to a Volatile Organic Mixture*. Washington: U.S. Environmental Protection Agency, 1992.

Humes, James C. *Instant Eloquence: A Lazy Man's Guide to Public Speaking*. New York: Harper & Row, 1973.

Jones, Clarence E. *After the Smoke Clears: Surviving the Police Shooting*. Springfield, Ill.: Thesis Press, 1989.

Kael, Pauline. *I Lost It at the Movies*. Boston: Little, Brown, 1965.

Keer, David W. *Restricted Activity Days and Other Problems Associated with Use of Marijuana Among Persons 18–44 Years of Age*. Hyattsville, Md.: U.S. Department of Health and Human Services.

Kingsolver, Barbara. *Pigs in Heaven.* New York: HarperCollins, 1993.

Knapp, Mary. *One Potato, Two Potato . . . : The Secret Education of American Children.* New York: Norton, 1976.

Korman, Gordon. *A Semester in the Life of a Garbage Bag.* New York: Scholastic, 1987.

Kuznetsov, Aleksei Pavlovich. *Ekologiia Donnykh Soobshchestv Shelfovykh Zon Microvogo Okeana: Troficheskaia Struktura Morskoi Donnoi Fauny.* Moskva: Nauka, 1980.

Lavine, Harold. *Smoke-Filled Rooms.* Englewood Cliffs, N.J.: Prentice-Hall, 1970.

Leonard, Michael. *I Would Have Saved Them if I Could.* New York: Farrar, Straus & Giroux, 1975.

Lesy, Michael. *Wisconsin Death Trip.* New York: Pantheon, 1973.

London, Manuel. *Career Management and Survival in the Workplace: Helping Employees Make Tough Career Choices, Stay Motivated, and Reduce Career Stress.* San Francisco: Jossey-Bass, 1987.

Loudis, Leonard A. *Skiing Out of Your Mind: The Psychology of Peak Performance.* Champaign, Ill.: Leisure Press, 1986.

McDonald, Megan. *The Potato Man.* New York: Orchard, 1991.

Money, John. *The Kaspar Hauser Syndrome of "Psychological Dwarfism."* Buffalo: Prometheus, 1992.

Montgomery, Robert Leo. *Memory Made Easy: The Complete Book of Memory Training.* New York: AMACOM, 1979.

National Institute of Health. *Check Your Smoking I.Q.* Bethesda: U.S. Department of Health and Human Services.

National Recreation and Park Association. *How to Remain Motivated When Those Around You Are Not. [sound recording.]* Louisville, Ky.: Meetings International, 1985.

Operation Weed and Seed Implementation Manual. Washington: U.S. Department of Justice, 1992.

Pantaleoni, C. A. *Handbook of Courtroom Demeanor and Testimony.* Englewood Cliffs, N.J.: Prentice-Hall, 1971.

Reed, Jean. *Resumes That Get Jobs.* New York: Prentice-Hall, 1992.

Reinfeld, Fred. *How to Use Algebra in Everyday Life.* London: Odhams Pr., Ltd., 1960.

Ross, Elizabeth Irvin. *How to Write While You Sleep—and Other Surprising Ways to Increase Your Writing Power.* Cincinnati, Ohio: Writer's Digest Books, 1985.

Salaman, Redcliffe N. *The History and Social Influence of the Potato.* Cambridge, England. Cambridge University Press, 1970.

Scheuer, Steven H., ed. *Movies on TV and Videocassette*. New York: Bantam, 1992.

Shenk, David, and Steve Silberman. *Skeleton Key: A Dictionary for Deadheads*. New York: Doubleday, 1994.

Shideler, Frank. *Potatoes for the Developing World: A Collaborative Experience*. Lima, Peru: International Potato Center, 1984.

Slack, Adrian. *Insect-Eating Plants and How to Grow Them*. Seattle: University of Washington Press, 1988.

Steinberg, Eve P. *You As a Law Enforcement Officer: Career Opportunities for a Secure Future*. New York: Arco, 1985.

Steincrohn, Peter Joseph. *How to be Lazy, Healthy, and Fit*. New York: Funk & Wagnalls, 1969.

Taubman, Paul, and Terence Wales. *Higher Education and Earnings: College As an Investment and a Screening Device*. New York: McGraw-Hill, 1974.

Telotte, J. P. *The Cult Film Experience: Beyond All Reason*. Austin: University of Texas Press, 1991.

Tisdell, Clement Allan. *Wild Pigs: Environmental Pest or Economic Resource?* Sydney: Pergamon, 1982.

Treffert, Daryl. *Extraordinary People: Understanding "Idiot Savants."* New York: Harper & Row, 1989.

Ullman, James Ramsey. *Where the Bong Tree Grows: The Log of One Man's Journey in the South Pacific*. Cleveland: World Publishing, 1963.

Ulrich, Seeliger, ed. *Coastal Plant Communities of Latin America*. San Diego: Academic Press, 1992.

U.S. Consumer Product Safety Commission. *High Chairs*. Washington: U.S. Consumer Product Safety Commission, 1990.

U.S. Department of Health and Human Services. *Drug Free for a New Century: Your Job and Mine*. Washington: U.S. Department of Health and Human Services, 1992.

Vash, Carolyn L. *The Burnt-Out Administrator*. New York: Springer, 1980.

Weil, Andrew. *From Chocolate to Morphine: Everything You Need to Know About Mind-Altering Drugs*. Boston: Houghton Mifflin, 1993.

Wexler, Michael, and John Hulme, eds. *Voices of the Xiled*. New York: Doubleday, 1994.

Appendix VIII
Competitor's Coupons

Some books enlighten. Some enlighten and entertain. And one book makes you a profit.

As you may have noticed, certain pizza chains have adopted the strategy of accepting all competitor's coupons in an effort to lure your business. Well, just because we don't agree with their politics doesn't mean we can't support our brothers and sisters in the fight for life.

Ladies and gentleman, BP Merchandising proudly announces an appendix more insidiously baked than any that has come before it: "Appendix VIII: Competitor's Coupons."

On the page that follows, behold: competitor's coupons for the Baked Potatoes Special: $2.99 large pie with one topping. (Carry-out only, just to be reasonable.)

If we assume that a normal large pie with one topping costs approximately $9.99, then with each use of a BP Competitor's Coupon you save $7.00 per pie for a total of $3 \times \$7.00 = \$21.00$. Enough to buy another copy of *Baked Potatoes* and still have change for all three large pies. That's right.

We're not talking pyramid scheme/*Seven Habits of Highly Effective People* improve-yourself-or-sell-dog-conditioner-make-you-money-in-ten-years make you money. We're talking actually, tangibly, pays you back for buying the book. When you damn well feel like getting paid.

Use them quietly and in good health.

Baked Potatoes in no way condones the use of competitor's coupons.

Acknowledgments

Ever since George Washington's mandate "Make the most of the hemp seed, sow it everywhere," select Americans in all eras and all trades, from college students and the unemployed to occasional commanders-in-chief, have risked life and liberty to fulfill this selfless and often consuming mission.

The authors gratefully acknowledge the hard-working patriots who have scoured the globe and sacrificed all to bring you *Baked Potatoes*:

BAKED POTATO ADVISORY COMMITTEE (BPAC):
Chairman: Ted Pryde
Terri Craft and *Juice* magazine
Dave from Dave's Videodrome
Kassi Day
Kim Eckhouse
Hadley Eure
Zach Hanner
Richard Hunt
Gideon Kendall
Kenyata and Pandora's Lunchbox
Miles MacQueen
John Marciano
Scott Moyers

Chris Pavone
Collins Roth
Diamond Mike Roth
Ellen Roth
Joe Roth
Bruce Tracy
Brent Watkins
Ann Wexler
Ilene Wexler
Philip Wexler

(BPDP)
Bo Webb

BAKED POTATO LEGAL DEFENSE TEAM:
Jed Alpert
Franklin Parlamis
Matthew Ryen
Anton Scalia

BAKED POTATO FOREIGN LOBBYISTS:
Hrundi V. Bakshi
Michael Goldberg

BAKED POTATO DEVELOPMENT:
VP of BP Development: Robbie
Schwartz
Development Executives:
Peter Glatzer
Jonas Pate
Josh Pate

Kristen Peace
Charlie Schulman

BAKED POTATO GENERAL:
Ari Wexler

BAKED POTATO MERCHANDISING:
Scott Kornfeld

BAKED AGENT:
Warren Frazier

RANDOM ACKNOWLEDGMENTS:
Bob and the Ale 'n' Wich
The White Rose System

Other High-Quality Projects from the Makers of Baked Potatoes

Vanishing Point: Below the surface of everyday life is "The Circuit"—a dangerous and exotic underground run by gypsy bands, hitchhikers, and wanderers. *Vanishing Point,* a twenty-six episode, digitally recorded audio experience, follows the adventures of two young men who enter this world by accident and will be lucky to escape with their lives.

As featured on twenty-five stations in the United States, Canada, and elsewhere, National Public Radio, *Radio & Records, College Music Journal,* winner Midwest Radio Theatre National Script Contest. Includes uncredited guest appearances.

"In the spirit, but not quite the fashion, of old-time radio serials, *Vanishing Point* offers a twisted, literate sense of adventure to the willing radio listener. A literal and figurative road-trip, the syndicated radio series follows Matt Gray and John Krane, desperado pilots of a beat-up Cadillac. With the help of a "bible to the road," the two encounter more than potholes on their excursions; the cosmic road map perpetually turns them toward mystical doorways and curious characters. Though the side roads they choose take them toward things unreal, all of this happens on America's open road. In one episode, Gray and Krane happen upon an infinite audio archive housed inside a roadside rib joint owned by Otis the Road Mystic. Since the team is always on the road headed toward something a tad off-center, *Vanishing Point* keeps its listeners fixed. The female narrator, who sounds as if she's taken her cues from a robotic phone-sex operator, also increases the seductive nature of the show. Her inflections when describing the smell of roasted pork inside the rib joint sound downright lascivious. The unforced dialogue, jabs at subcultures and twists on stoic radio dramas and geeky sci-fi drivel, make for a sophisticated program. *Vanishing Point* makes room at the end and sometimes in the middle for musical guest appearances" —Steve Ciabattoni, *College Music Journal.*

You will not be disappointed.

Untitled

After a year of sampling the best and worst of our world's giant stoned-viewing buffet, the authors of *Baked Potatoes,* in close association with the BPDP, the Baked Potato General, and the BP Legal Defense Team, bring you a movie that, unlike so many others that say they are like no other, is *really* like no other.

What's inside is an artifact privy only to those with the faith to find out. Let us just say, as we have at other times in this text, and we don't say it lightly: You will not be disappointed.

No misguided producers. No budget constraints. No concern for the adverse effects of violence and "other" subject matter on the minds of the masses. No boundaries, no mercy, no food, no rhyme, no reason, nolo contendere.

If you like *Baked Potatoes* and its somewhat "revisionist" take on the Seder plate of life, you'll like this movie. The lamb shank, the bitter herbs, the egg, it's all there . . . and prepared specifically for the needs of the Baked Potato.

We did our best to bring you the goods.

Strong enough for the sober but made for the stoned. The really stoned.

Available through The LodesTone Catalog: 1-800-411-MIND.

Voices of the Xiled: *(Michael Wexler & John Hulme, eds. Doubleday. U.S. $14.95/Canada $19.95)*

"What they came up with is an exhilaratingly diverse and honest collection of short fiction by 20 young writers. Although the voices in this collage are undeniably unique, certain themes bind the stories together: a search for self; innocence and experience; slow-dripping desperation; discontent; disillusionment; restlessness; altered states of consciousness. These writers, both new and established, have mined the margins where the psyche begins to fray. From the haunting voice of a baby not yet conceived in Tamara Jeffries's 'Black Tea,' to the scathingly bizarre sick puppy in David Foster Wallace's 'Girl with Curious Hair,' (a fitting cellmate for Alex in Anthony Burgess's *A Clockwork Orange)" —Publishers Weekly*.

"They've selected stories with no agenda in mind—except that they didn't want to have an agenda. Throughout, people are putting themselves back together after the likes of childhood abuse (Nicole Cooley's 'The Photograph Album') and memory loss (Mitch Berman's 'Wabi'). Others are self-destructing in the false perfection suburbia (Chris Hallman's 'Utopia Road') . . . every voice is strong, moving, and meaningful" —*Kirkus Reviews*.

Available at your local bookstore.

John Hulme and Michael Wexler are productive members of society and are active in myriad church, synagogue, and mosque groups as well as volunteering their time for the annual Baked Olympics.

While not exercising, eating healthy, or canvassing local residents in a futile effort to sell Bob Ross–like oil paintings, they devote their energies primarily to doing nothing and working on their critically acclaimed "Baked" series. Whether is be *Baked Potatoes: A Pot Smoker's Guide to Film and Video* or *Baked Alaska: An Eskimo's Guide to the Pastry Labyrinth*, the authors consistently put their Michigan and Princeton educations to good use.

Hulme and Wexler grew up in Highland Park, New Jersey, and were friends in high school. Now they hate each other.

THE WHITE HOUSE

WASHINGTON

March 6, 1995

Baked Potatoes
Post Office Box 2208
Wilmington, North Carolina 28402

Dear Friends:

Thank you for your kind invitation to President Clinton. He
does appreciate your offer and is sorry he will be unable to
accept.

Unfortunately, the tremendous demands on the President as he
works to move our country forward do not give him the opportunity
to accept as many invitations as he would like.

On behalf of the President, thank you again for your
invitation. Your continued interest and support are deeply
appreciated.

Sincerely,

William M. Webster, IV
Director of Scheduling and Advance

WMW/ine

BAKED Potatoes

goes on-line

Why stop the madness once you've read the book?

You're still getting high.

So are we.

And since it seems that everyone today has a Web site—
you've probably got a Web site yourself—
now *Baked Potatoes* will be frying
on the World Wide Web.

Exchange baked ideas, meet friends, have a cigar.
Interact, chat, revel in your addiction, get help,
post, read, write, vote on the merits and demerits of the classics.
Check out reviews of new releases.
See the thing called SonicNet.
Sample our collection of bestiality stills.
Just kidding.
Maybe.
Seek and
download the BP Treasure Map and clues.

Witness the fruits of sick people, inexplicably given a chance to explore
their malady in the public arena.

Check it out before the government reads this page and shuts us down.

BAKED Potatoes
on SONICNET

http://www.sonicnet.com/baked